<u>זיכ‬רון עולם‬</u>

For an Eternal Memory:
Ordinary and Unusual Jewish Cemetery
Monuments and How to Create Them

By Joshua L. Segal, Rabbi

8/5/2013

Jewish Cemetery Publishing, LLC, Nashua, NH USA

Cover Photo:
Prague Old Jewish Cemetery
By Stephen Borko
For more information:
http://stephenborkophotographs.com

i

לזכר עולם

For an Eternal Memory:
Ordinary and Unusual Jewish Cemetery Monuments and How to Create Them

- - - - -

By Joshua L. Segal, Rabbi

© Copyright 2009: JCP, LLC
31 Scott Avenue
Nashua, NH 03062-2443
Email: SegalJL@aol.com
Web: CemeteryJewish.com

Hebrew Fonts: HebraicaII and NewJerusalem are licensed by Jewish Cemetery Publishing, LLC from "Linguistic Software."

978-0-9764057-4-0

ISBN 978-0-9764057-4-0

90000 >

9 780976 405740

Other publications from "Jewish Cemetery Publications, LLC"

A Self-Guided Tour of the Temple Beth Abraham Cemetery, Nashua, NH, ©2001.

A Self-Guided Tour of the Adath Israel Cemetery, Massena, New York, ©2002.

The Old Jewish Cemetery of Newport, A Visitor's Guide to Viewing the Cemetery, © 2007 ISBN 0-9764057-0-9

A Field Guide to Visiting a Jewish Cemetery, ©2005, ISBN 0-9764057-1-7

The Old Jewish Cemetery of Newport, A History of North America's Oldest Extant Jewish Cemetery, ©2007 ISBN 0-9764057-2-5

A Self-Guided Tour of Monuments of Jews Buried in the Mount Auburn Cemetery Cambridge, Massachusetts: A History of the Evolution of the Jewish Presence in America's Oldest Garden Cemetery ©2007 ISBN 0-9764057-3-3

Cemeteries as Museums

Jewish Cemetery Publications, LLC will create booklets (such as some of the self-guided tours listed above) which will turn your local Jewish cemetery into a museum of local Jewish history.

To place an order or for more information or pricing, contact:

Jewish Cemetery Publishing, LLC
31 Scott Avenue
Nashua, NH 03062-2443

or

Email: <SegalJL@aol.com>
Web: CemeteryJewish.com

Preface

My book, *A Field Guide to Visiting a Jewish Cemetery* was written to provide the opportunity for a visitor to:

1. Understand iconography,
2. Understand most of the Hebrew with little more than a rudimentary knowledge of "prayer book Hebrew"
3. Have some appreciation of cemetery etiquette.
4. Have some idea of the breadth of options that one might find for epitaphs.

Because of that content, the book has become popular in many communities, including genealogists, cemetery owners, Jewish educators and cemetery hobbyists of all sorts.

However, for individuals contemplating how they want to be remembered this volume is intended to fill in three major gaps not covered in *A Field Guide ...* First, this book outlines a step-by-step process to select and design a monument that will be a worthy memorial to someone's life. Second, it provides an extensive section on the things one can do to make a monument unique within the accepted rules of the cemetery in which one will be buried. And third, it gives a description with examples, of the juxtaposition of names and monuments over which most have no control.

There is rarely a time that I visit a new cemetery that I don't find material that is interesting, different and could or should be included in this book. But there comes a time where one has to stop and move on.

Those who enjoy visiting cemeteries may find it worthwhile to check out the website of "The Association for Gravestone Studies (AGS)." AGS is on the web at: http://www.gravestonestudies.org.

Table of Contents

Acknowledgements

I acknowledge the following people who provided inputs:

Rabbi Hillel Cohn, who provided both photos and background stories for the entries from "House of Eternity, San Bernardino, CA."

Dan Lynch, who provided the photograph of the white bronze monument shown later and inputs on "erratics".

Bruce Leon for the entry and background story on his ancestor from the "Old Jewish Cemetery, Waldheim Cemetery, Forest Park, IL."

Ms. Elisa Ho, Mr. Kevin Proffitt and Dr. Gary Zola of the American Jewish Archives, Cincinnati, OH for the information on the tombstone of I. M. Wise.

Karin Sprague of "Karin Sprague Stone Carvers", URL: http://www.karinsprague.com for her permission to use a photo of her work showing the "hands of the priest".

Tomek Wisniewski, Bialystok, Poland, for permission to use an example of a wooden monument from his article "Wooden *Matzevot*", published on-line at "http://www.jewishmag.com/127mag/wooden_tombsto nes/wooden_tombstones.htm".

Moises Reyes, Supervisor of Maintenance at Beth David Cemetery, Hollywood, FL for taking me to a variety of interesting monuments.

Abigail S. Malis for the photo of the "Tomb of the Lost Sailors" from the Herzl Cemetery, Jerusalem.

Rabbi Howard Kosovske for reviewing and commenting on the manuscript.

Steve Borko for providing the cover photo. For more of Steve's work, see http://stephenborkophotographs.com.

Judy Fox for the all of the entries associated with the NJ cemeteries mentioned; for her reading, editing and countless other superb suggestions.

Karen Satz, my wife, who has been my editor and a constant source of inputs to this work.

Introduction

What is the purpose of a cemetery? Cemeteries are mini-museums. Of course, a cemetery is a place that is a repository for human remains, and a place to memorialize those buried in them. But they have also become a *de facto* museum of a very special type of art in the form of cemetery monuments.

The name of the memorial to the Holocaust in Jerusalem is *Yad Vashem* (Isaiah 56:5, *inter alia*) often translated "a memorial and a name", but literally, *"Yad Vashem"* translates to "a hand and a name". The "name" part on most cemetery monuments is simple. Consider the monument that follows: The name part is: Mitchell Rubin, Born: 1916 Died: 1997.

To understand the *"yad"* part, (i.e. "hand" or "memorial") we look to the Psalms which state: "establish the work of our hands (Psalms 90:17)." On some level for the monument to be a memorial it needs to communicate something about "the work of our hands", specifically who was the person behind the name? And that is what is missing from the monument below:

Adath Israel, Massena, NY

1

This book is intended for many audiences including the following:

1. If you are contemplating your own mortality and are thinking about how you want to be remembered by a passerby in another 100 years, Section 1 of this book will give you a road map to design your own monument that will provide a meaningful memorial and perhaps, even be written about! Appendix A provides a "monument designer's checklist." What's more, Section 2 will give you an idea of what to be careful of, the importance of editing and the uncontrollable coincidences that one can't plan for. Section 3 is a combination of a summary, exceptions and things that just didn't fit into the earlier sections.

2. If you are in the position of designing a monument for someone else and recognize that this is more than a perfunctory responsibility, this will book will allow you to transform a "*Shem* (a name)" into a "*Yad Vashem* (a memorial)."

3. If you are a cemetery hobbyist, the kind of person whose car would be equipped with the bumper sticker, "I Brake for Old Graveyards," this book is for you. But I suspect for that kind of person, any book on cemeteries would do!

4. And if you are the type of person who just enjoys funny things, Section 2 will offer you humorous sayings, iconography and errors, in a context in which you might not have expected to find humor.

- - - - -

Monuments (Hebrew: *Ma-tsei-vah* – מצבה) are a custom, not a requirement of Jewish law. Some suggest that the practice was begun by Jacob, when he set up a pillar on Rachel's grave (Genesis 35:20). Many reasons are offered for the placing of a monument, but the most common is to mark the spot for future visits by friends and relatives of the deceased.

The subtitle of this book, "Ordinary and Unusual Jewish Cemetery Monuments and How to Create Them" might cause some a problem citing Psalm 49[1] and other sources which suggest that we are all equal in death. By this standard, all monuments should be the same or similar. And there are certain cemeteries whose rules encourage and even enforce this kind of conformity. The truth of the matter is that Jewish cemeteries from Orthodox to the most liberal have monuments that include inscriptions of every imaginable length, monuments of every imaginable size and artwork from minimal iconography to museum quality art.

The next few examples in this chapter are offered to help provide a context, the breadth of opportunities that people have taken to assure themselves a "*Yad Vashem,*" a lasting memorial.

Many monuments give us no insight into the person buried there, beyond name, dates and a standard epitaph. The photo below is an example where the person symbolically lays out his tombstone as a ledger page with the names of his survivors in the ledger!

---

[1] Psalm 49:18 For when he dies he shall carry nothing away; his glory shall not go down after him.

ACCOUNT NO. 32 M. MURRY WAYNER			DATE OPENED JULY 4, 1920 DATE CLOSED NOV. 25, 19??
Names	Interest	Personal acct.	Credits
SYLVIA	LOVE	WIFE	
STEPHEN ALAN	LOVE	SON	
BARRY LEE	LOVE	SON	
ROSE	LOVE	MOTHER	
JOSEPH	LOVE	FATHER	
MILDRED	LOVE	SISTER	

Mt. Nebo, Miami, FL

Occasionally someone will take the time to write something extensive. Sometimes, it is a description of the individual's accomplishments, sometimes it is about the individual's survivors, and sometimes it is a quote from the Bible or other literature giving us insight into the person and the person's life.

The following tombstone includes the epitaph: *LIVE-LOVE-LAUGH*. The epitaph may be based on the song, "When the Red, Red, Robin Comes Bob, Bob Bobbin' Along" written by Harry Woods which includes the words, *"Live, love, laugh..."*.

WALTERS

BELOVED HUSBAND - FATHER GRANDFATHER & LOYAL FRIEND
HAROLD R.
OCT. 22, 1910 — NOV. 10, 1996

BELOVED WIFE-MOTHER AND GRANDMOTHER
MADELYN G.
AUG. 12, 1917 — AUG. 6, 1981

LIVE- LOVE - LAUGH

Star of David, Fort Lauderdale, FL

4

There are very few inscriptions that truly generate a belly laugh. But in a world where so many of our lives are given meaning by our families and friends, career and *mitsvot*, there is something special about those inscriptions that go in a different direction.

I was going to suggest that cemetery studies are not "rocket science" but then I found the following with a picture of the space shuttle in the lower left:

Emanu El, San Bernardino, CA

Perhaps he worked on the Space Shuttle and/or he saw the shuttle as his personal conveyance to his heavenly home (the *o-lam ha-ba*).

- - - - -

One observation that I've made is that tombstones that are intentionally funny are relatively recent and are becoming more common. Perhaps it is a reflection that our society and our standard of living have made life so much more pleasant than ever before. Therefore, we are willing to reflect on the deceased with an appreciation that they had good lives. And when visiting the cemetery, the use of humor allows us to keep the focus on the upbeat aspects of the lives we are remembering.

5

Section 1.
Ideas and Info for those Designing a Tombstone

Too many people take the "plain vanilla standard monuments" and forget to examine the alternatives available.
The purpose of this section is to provide the reader with a
step-by-step method to contemplate the many options
available. The least expensive markers, monuments, *ma-
tsei-vot,* etc. start at about $1000 (value of US dollars
based on ca. 2010 CE) and go up from there.

Appendix A offers a checklist for someone contemplating
the design of a monument either for themselves or on
behalf of someone else.

Monument Format
Here are the issues to be considered[2].

1. Decoration
2. Introductory Line
3. Name Line
4. Date (including Information on the age of
    the deceased)
5. Epitaph

- - - - -

The monument of my mother, Mollie Segal, is used as the
paradigm for this chapter.

---

[2] The material is extracted from the chapter, Cemeteries 101 from *A
Field Guide to Visiting a Jewish Cemetery*, by Rabbi Joshua Segal,
©2005, JCP, LLC, NH

אמנו היקרה
מלכה בת
חיים ושרה ,
נפ׳ כ״א טבת תשנ״ח
MOLLIE SEGAL
DIED JANUARY 19, 1998
ת׳ נ׳ צ׳ ב׳ ה׳

Adath Israel, Massena, NY

The Standard Decorations:

The **six-pointed star** known as the Star of David, the *Magen David*, or the Jewish Star is one of the best known symbols of Judaism. It is the most common decoration on contemporary Jewish monuments.

The ***menorah*** or candelabrum appears on some women's monuments. The lighting of candles is a commandment (*mitsvah*) specifically designated for a woman to perform. Monuments show these candelabras with two, three, four, five or seven branches.

For those who claim to be direct descendants from the *ko-ha-nim,* כהנים, "the Biblical priests," **the hands** are shown at the top of the monument in the position in which they are held when the Priestly Benediction (Numbers 6:24-26) is offered.

8

Sometimes the letters: פ"נ pronounced: *Po nik-bar (nik-be-ra)* meaning "Here lies," also appear as part of the decoration as shown in both the *Magen David* and the *menorah* below.

Magen David

Hands

Menorah

In our paradigm shown below, the decoration is the *Magen David*, with the פ"נ separated by the decoration. The use of abbreviation marks varies greatly from monument to monument and it is shown in the example as פ'נ'.

Many of the less common decorations and options are shown in the various chapters of Section 2.

9

Introductory Line

The standard "Introductory Line" is a simple declaration of survivor's relationship to the deceased. This line sometimes may not appear at all. Examples of the "Introductory Line" include:

My beloved father	*A-vi ha-ya-kar*	אבי היקר
Our beloved father	*A-vi-nu ha-ya-kar*	אבינו היקר
My beloved mother	*I-mi ha-yi-ka-ra*	אמי היקרה
Our beloved mother	*I-mei-nu ha-yi-ka-ra*	אמנו היקרה
My beloved wife	*Ish-ti ha-yi-ka-ra*	אשתי היקרה
My beloved husband	*ba-a-li ha-ya-kar*	בעלי היקר

Some very common "introductory lines" strings two nouns strung together:

My beloved wife and our beloved mother	*Ish-ti ve-i-mei-nu ha-ye-ka-ra*	אשתי ואמנו היקרה
My beloved husband and our beloved father.	*Ba-a-li ve-a-vi-nu ha-ya-kar*	בעלי ואבינו היקר

In the paradigm, shown again below, the introductory line is:

"Our beloved mother, *I-mei-nu ha-yi-ka-ra*, אמנו היקרה."

10

Name line simplest syntax:

The common name syntax is shown below:

a.   b.   c.   d.   e.   f.   g.

Here lies <title><name><son/daughter of> <title> <parent's name> <last name>

a. Here lies. (Masc.)   *Po nik-bar*   פה נקבר   פ"נ

     Here lies. (Fem.)   *Po nik-be-ra* פה נקברה   פ"נ

     (Often omitted here if included in decoration.)

b. Title [Sometimes omitted]

     Mister   *reb*   רב   ר'

     Mrs.   *ma-rat*   מרת   מ' or מר'

c. Name of the deceased:

A middle name may also be included, but it is not in our paradigm. The name in our paradigm is "Malkah, מלכה", which corresponds precisely to the English name, Mollie.

d. Relationship (Son/Daughter of...)

     Son of   *Ben*   בן

     Son of Mister ...   *Ben reb (Bar)* בן רב   בר'

     Daughter of   *Bat*   בת

     Daughter of Mister *Bat reb (Bar)* בת רב   בר'

     In our paradigm above, Mollie, "Daughter of (i.e. Bat, בת)."

e. Title of parent:

     The titles of the parent are exactly the same as the titles of the deceased and were described in b., above.

     In our paradigm, there are no titles.

f. Parent's name:
Traditionally, the only parent mentioned on the monuments was the father. This is still the case in most Orthodox cemeteries. Reform and some Conservative cemeteries now include both the father and mother's name. This is the case in our paradigm, which identifies "Malkah as the daughter of Chaim and Sarah."

g. Last name (surname):
The last name is usually a transliteration. It often does not appear at all or may stand alone on the following line. In our paradigm, it does not appear.

Dates

Generic Example:
a.   b.   c.   d.   d.   c.   b.   a.
Died \<day>\<month>\<year>   \<year>\<month>\<day> 'נכ

Specific paradigm:
        d.   c.   b.   a.

ח"נשת תבט א"כ 'פנ

a. b. c. d.   d.   c.   b.   a.
Died 21 Tevet 5758   ח"נשת תבט א"כ 'פנ

This paradigm doesn't include something to indicate the age of the deceased. In most monuments in American Jewish cemeteries, a date of birth is given as a common calendar date.

See Table 1 for days, Table 2 for Months.

Table 1: days

1	א'	11	י"א	21	כ"א
2	ב'	12	י"ב	22	כ"ב
3	ג'	13	י"ג	23	כ"ג
4	ד'	14	י"ד	24	כ"ד
5	ה'	15	ט"ו	25	כ"ה
6	ו'	16	ט"ז	26	כ"ו
7	ז'	17	י"ז	27	כ"ז
8	ח'	18	י"ח	28	כ"ח
9	ט'	19	י"ט	29	כ"ט
10	י'	20	כ'	30	ל'

Table 2: months

Tishri	תשרי	Adar Bet	אדר ב'
Cheshvan	חשון	Nisan	נסן
Kislev	כסלו	Iyar	אייר
Tevet	טבת	Sivan	סיון
Shevat	שבט	Tammuz	תמוז
Adar	אדר	Av	אב
Adar Aleph	אדר א'	Elul	אלול

Epitaph

Epitaphs can be long and complicated. However, a large plurality of monuments has the following epitaph.

Let his (her) soul	*Te-hi naf-sho*	תנצב"ה
be bound up	*(naf-sha) tsa-ro-ra*	
in the bonds of the living.	*bi-tse-ror ha-cha-yim.*	
(Adapted from1 Sam. 25:29)[3]		

---

[3] Note: The Hebrew acronym doesn't change in a multi-person monument. The English becomes "Let their souls …"; and the Hebrew becomes, "*Te-hi naf-sho-tei-hem tse-ru-rot…*"

Many Jews believe in the concept of "life after death" or a "World to Come".   However, from the point of view of Jewish theology, there are no guarantees.   The only guarantee is that we will be remembered by the living for those things we did in our lifetimes.   This is the message reflected in the acronym תנצב״ה.

In the paradigm for this chapter, this example of the epitaph is shown next:

- - - - -

Epitaphs, editing and other issues will be covered in many of the chapters that follow.   The remainder of this section covers a number of options including font choice, material choice and shape; and even how the limitations of "perpetual care" might impact one's choices. There are also many wonderful options for decorations. And when deciding on a headstone, the question of whether to select a single headstone or a double headstone for husband and wife is also discussed.

Section 1, Chapter 1. Materials for Monuments

Materials That are Usually Permitted
As a category, permitted materials tend to be those that will last and that are relatively easy to maintain.

Granite
Granite is the most common material in today's cemeteries. It is available in many colors and many finishes. It is extremely durable and has been become the stone of choice for most monuments. It began to be popular in the late 19th century as the tools to cut it, carve it and/or sandblast it became available.

Erratic
An erratic is a large amorphous local stone, often left by a glacier which leaves the rock's edges rounded. They can be of many sizes. The massive example below is larger than allowed in most new cemeteries. These may be carved, or sandblasted; or in the case below, a metallic plate with the family name, is attached to the stone. One must wonder how these massive rocks are moved. One was so large, the caretaker told me, that the flat-bed truck buckled during its unloading.

Grove Street, West Roxbury, MA

Miscellaneous Local Stones

The example that follows was quarried and shaped to look like a bear. But because it was so unconventional, it required special approval from the cemetery before it was placed.

Adath Yeshurun, France St., Minneapolis. MN

Rose Quartz

A number of varieties of quartz are used. In most cases, one surface is flattened and a brass plaque is affixed to it. Of the quartzes, rose is the most popular.

Mohlover, Baker St., West Roxbury, MA

Slate

Slate has been used for centuries. It is extremely difficult to engrave. As a result, slate monuments tend to be both expensive and even for those who can afford slate; it is hard to find artisans who work in this medium. Slate is a sedimentary material which means that it forms in layers. Sometimes, there are flaws internal to the slates that are not obvious when quarried. As a result, if and when slate deteriorates, it usually delaminates. However, if it doesn't delaminate, it is virtually indestructible. Slates from churchyards dating to the 17th century are as readable today as they were when they were carved.

One of the best carvers of modern slate monuments is Karin Sprague of "Karin Sprague Stone Carvers", URL: http://www.karinsprague.com. An example of her work with the "hands of the priest" is shown next. The Hebrew above the star, חבר שלום, is translated "good-bye friend." It became popular after President Bill Clinton's spoke those words to Yitschak Rabin at the funeral, following Rabin's assassination in 1995.

Brass or Other Metallic Markers

In many cases, monuments are composites of a stone with a metallic marker attached to it. One of the biggest problems with metallic markers is that they have become a target for thieves as the value of scrap metal has gone up. Some argue that this is a new problem. However, it is not! There is a monument from the 18th century in the Colonial Cemetery in Newport, RI that is in beautiful condition, but no one is sure who is buried there. It was reported to have had a lead plaque with an inscription that was stolen (or salvaged), during the Civil War to use for a cannon ball[4].

Metallic monuments as a class tend to have less interesting epitaphs, but as the example below shows, that is not a limitation of the medium.

Linwood, Randolph, MA

---

[4] *The Old Jewish Cemetery of Newport, A History of North America's Oldest Extant Jewish Cemetery*, Joshua Segal, JCP, LLC, NH ©2007 pg. 141

Mixed Stones

Sometimes combinations of materials are used. The specific example shown next is where the monument is made of two very different-colored pieces of granite which gives a very striking effect.

Minneapolis Hebrew, Minneapolis

Materials that are not Usually Permitted at Many Cemeteries Today

It should be noted that at most cemeteries there are limitations on monument size as well as monument materials. Part of the reasoning for the limitations is that cemetery owners and managers are concerned with *ke-vod ha-meit* (honoring the deceased). As such, they understand that the cemetery, not the family, will ultimately have to maintain the monuments. So restrictions are in place to deal with issues of maintenance as well as the consequences of vandalism on the larger monuments.

Wrought Iron

The unusual monument that follows has the letters applied more as an appliqué than etched or carved. Notice how over the years, parts of letters have fallen off and there are clearly some rust issues.

Beth Joseph 2, Woburn, MA

Note: The next to last line reads "Vermont (ווערמאנט)". It is odd that someone from Vermont, America's largest provider of stone cemetery monuments, would have a wrought iron marker!

Limestone or Marble

Older monuments tended to be limestone or marble. They are soft stones and very easy to carve. However, the properties that make them easy to carve, also make them subject to the elements in general and acid rain in particular. Here is an example from the tombstone of Isaac Touro, died 1784 from the Old Colonial Cemetery, Newport, RI.

While the above example shows a readable stone, many 100-year old marble monuments are unreadable.

Wood

Wood as a material for a monument is perfectly acceptable[5]. It suffers the same problem as marble, namely durability. As a result, many cemeteries ban wooden monuments because they represent a maintenance problem, not because they are Jewishly unacceptable.

There were many wooden monuments in the Jewish cemeteries of Europe but not one survived the vandalism of the holocaust. An example of a prewar photograph of a wooden monument from Radom, Poland follows[6].

The monument inscription reads:

Translation	Transcription
Here lies ? Ruth Hinda	פ"נ ? רות הינדא
? daughter of Mr. Shlomo Tsvi?, may his light shine,	(? בר') שלמה צ?י נ"י
Goldring	גאלדרינג
Died 16 Tei-veit 5701 (Jan. 14, 1941)	נפ' ט"ז טבת תש"א

Radom, Poland

[5] http://data.ccarnet.org/cgi-bin/respdisp.pl?file=183&year=narr or New American Reform Responsa, Walter Jacob, 1992.
[6] "Wooden *Matzevot*", by Tomek Wisniewski, Bialystok, Poland. "http://www.jewishmag.com/127mag/wooden_tombstones/wooden_to mbstones.htm" (published on-line) Used with author's permission.

Zinc, (also known as White Bronze)

The zinc monument was popular in the early 20th century. There are no longer any manufacturers of zinc monuments within the United States. Looking at the photo of the Pomeranch monument, dated 1898, it looks almost like a granite monument. The easy way to tell the difference is: 1) the zinc has a bluish hue and 2) if you thump it, it gives off a hollow metallic sound.

Pittsfield, MA

Other Materials

Other materials include sandstone, schist, local stones of all sorts, various composite stones, concrete and even petrified wood. Given today's technology, the key question in deciding monument materials is durability and esthetics. Sandstone, composites, as well as concrete, tend to be porous inviting lichen growth and erosion. Petrified wood is hard to find.

Section 1, Chapter 2. Shapes of Monuments

In considering monument shape, one must check the cemetery rules and bylaws, which in recent years have become more and more restrictive. Some mandate specific sizes; some mandate specific shapes.

Numerous examples of unusual shapes are shown through this volume including obelisks, spheres, tree trunks, angels, animal shapes, etc.

Monument Tops

Many of the monument tops shown and described below are generic cemetery art rather than specifically Jewish cemetery art. In some cemeteries they are common. In others, there are no monument tops.

A. Acorn	B. Ball	C. Jug (or Urn)
An acorn becomes a great oak only after it is buried. It symbolizes afterlife.	A ball is the perfect shape with no beginning and no end, symbolizing eternity.	The jug is symbolic of the body which is the container for the eternal soul.

The veiled urn or jug is shown next. Some suggest that the veil is a symbol of mourning. Others would say, the cloth is symbolic that the work of life is incomplete and partially hidden (or veiled). It is not generally a Jewish symbol although it frequently appears in Jewish cemeteries as do the other monument tops. It could be mistaken for or used as a Levitic pitcher, but that is a stretch.

Knights of Liberty, Woburn, MA

Teardrop or Candle Flame?

The monument below can be interpreted to be either a candle flame with the symbolism being "eternal light" or a teardrop indicating sorrow for the loss of the deceased.

Regardless of which was intended, the monument stands out beautifully as a contrast to the more standard shapes.

United Jewish Brotherhood, Minneapolis, MN

Irregular Shapes of All Sorts

Other common shapes include hearts, the ten command-ments and a variety of irregular shapes. Many are shown in other chapters. A couple follow, but the options for shape are limitless:

Temple Beth Abraham, Nashua, NH   Anshe Sefard, Baker Street, West Roxbury, MA

Section 1, Chapter 3. Double Headstones

Unless both partners of a couple are elderly and unlikely to remarry, I strongly suggest avoiding the double monument for the reasons outlined in this chapter.

The Empty Gravesite

What follows is the classic example of the empty grave. Mr. Kaufman passed more than 50-years ago and it is unlikely that his spouse is still alive or will ever be buried here. We can hypothesize any of the following:

1. She remarried and is buried elsewhere. While there is a tradition that suggests widows and widowers be buried with their first spouse, the empirical evidence shows otherwise.

2. She is buried there, but her survivors never got around to adding her inscription. This occurs infrequently, but it occurs.

3. The family and/or the spouse relocated and they chose to bury that person in their new community.

United Jewish Brotherhood, Minneapolis, MN

Regardless of the reason, the empty inscription is esthetically unappealing.

29

When the Author of the First Epitaph is Unavailable or Unwilling to provide the Second

The next two monuments are examples where one spouse survived the other by more than a decade. We can assume that whoever wrote the first inscription is not available to write a matching inscription. The result in both cases is a double stone where the inscriptions are very unbalanced.

<u>Long Epitaph – Short Epitaph</u>
Notice in the monument below, Bessie passes away almost 13-years after Max. The imbalance in the length of their respective epitaphs is esthetically problematic.

A careful look also shows the fonts used are not the same. Two problems play out in this monument. First, whoever wrote Max's epitaph was not available to write Bessie's. So if despite my warnings you choose to have a double stone, before the stone is manufactured, make sure a format has been decided for both sides and pre-compose a parallel epitaph. And second, monument manufacturers come and go. Font sets vary from manufacturer to manufacturer, so even if all the epitaphs are written in advance, matching the lettering can still be a problem.

Temple Beth Abraham, Nashua, NH

Trying to match an acrostic.

The following double headstone is an example of trying to match the format of the two sides of a monument. In this case, Pesach predeceased Trina by 15 years. The left side is a regular acrostic spelling out the name, *Pesach* with the first letter of the first word of each of the 3-lines of the inscription. Compare this with the right side. The woman's name, *Trina*, is spelled out vertically in the right column. However, the letters of her name are not the first letters of the first words of each line. In this case, I would categorize the inscriptions as esthetically balanced but grammatically interesting.

Tiffereth Israel of Winthrop, Everett, MA

31

פ'נ'

<table>
<tr><td></td><td>1.</td></tr>
<tr><td>פַּאר ראשנו זקן ושבע</td><td>2.</td></tr>
<tr><td>סַתר מעשיו צדקה עשה</td><td>3.</td></tr>
<tr><td>חַסיד וְיֹרֵשׁ אבינו היקר</td><td>4.</td></tr>
<tr><td>רי פסח אליהו</td><td>5.</td></tr>
<tr><td>בֹּרֹ ישראל משה</td><td>6.</td></tr>
</table>

נפטר כ"ג אדר א' תרצֹה
תנצב"ה

פ ט אמנו היקרה
ר אשה תמימה וישרה
יי אשת חיל עקרת הבית
נ יראת ה' וחוננת דלים
א ה' טריינא בת ר' צבי
נפטרה י' חשון תשי"א
תנצב"ה

Beloved husband and father	Beloved mother
Pesach	Trina
Died Feb. 26, 1935	Died Oct. 21, 1950
Age 80 YRS	Age 83 YRS

GROMAN

Translation:
Here lie

Pe The glory of our old and aged leader:
Sa He performed quiet deeds of charity.
Ch Righteous and God fearing (וְיֹרֵשׁ)
was our beloved father,

Mr. Pe-sach Ei-li-ya-hu

son of Mr. Yis-ra-eil Mo-she.

Died 23 A-dar 1 5695
Let his soul...

T Our beloved mother:
R a perfect and upright woman,
I a woman of valor, the
mistress of her home,

N a fearer of God (ה'),
who favored the
downtrodden,

A the woman (ה'), Trina
daughter of Mr. Tsvi.
Died 10 Chesh-van 5711
Let her soul...

32

Over and Under

In the photo shown below, there are two examples of "over and under" inscriptions. Both are double-wide monuments, clearly intended for two people. The one in the back, William and Irene Basser, is complete. But the one in front looks balanced and appropriate, even though there is likely a missing name.

The problem with the "over and under" inscriptions is figuring out who is buried on the left and/or right, although this is easily solved with a footstone.

Cedar Park, Paramus, NJ

Filing Jointly
The following double monument, with two stacked cubes, for Irwin and Rebecca Small shows something different in double monuments. On the left is a cameo photo of the two of them, probably their wedding photo. At the bottom of the photo is an inset showing the details of the inscription and on the right is a detail inset of the cute way they give their wedding anniversary date (Filed Jointly Since 11-28-37), indicating a 66-year marriage.

Clearly, this monument fits this book's sub-title "... Unusual ... Cemetery Monuments and How to Create Them." The down side: this monument could have appeared in any cemetery and no one would know those buried there were Jewish. There is no Hebrew and no Jewish iconography.

Hebrew Section, Monadnock View, Keene, NH

Section 1, Chapter 4. Font Choices and Language

The choice of fonts can really change the look of the monument and many overlook this choice. Given today's technology, modern monuments are not limited by a few font sets that a specific monument manufacturer might have available.

Raised or lowered Lettering
The example that follows has the Hebrew letters cut into the monument and the English inscription with raised lettering.

Tupper Lake, NY

35

Cursive

The mixing of the cursive font with the block English and the Hebrew has a nice effect.

United Jewish Brotherhood, Minneapolis

But be careful if legibility is a concern! However, what we see next is a signature. Perhaps, it is a subtle way of "signing out" from life!

United Jewish Brotherhood, Minneapolis

Other Fonts

The composite shown below gives a perspective on the breadth of opportunities available to enhance a monument, by merely selecting a font set or multiple font sets.

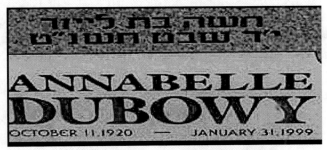

Colma, CA

Language

In general, Jews have embraced the vernacular as their
"physical" language, while retaining Hebrew as their
"spiritual" language. Additional languages do appear on
tombstones in the United States but usually, only for the
first generation immigrants, who, in many cases, either
never learned English or for whom English was a second
language.

37

For many immigrant Jews, their first language was Yiddish. Because of the cultural impact of Yiddish on American Judaism, we might expect Yiddish to be an exception in the grand scheme of language usage on tombstones. However, by the late twentieth century, most Jews no longer spoke Yiddish. Despite this, Yiddish vocabulary and Yiddishisms are still infused as a major part of American Jewish culture. Still, a trip though cemeteries will show that for most Jews, Yiddish is not found on their tombstones beyond the first generation.

There is one vestige of Yiddish that remains. Many "Hebrew names" are not Hebrew at all but European names transliterated into Yiddish, such as "Brina – ברײנא" or Hebrew names that have been "Yiddishized" such as "Yo-seph (Joseph) coming out as "Yossel – יאסל." When these names appear, they often use the rules for Yiddish vocalization which are different from Hebrew.

For many Sephardic Jews (Jews of Spanish descent), Judeo-Spanish, (also known as Ladino or Espanol,) was their first language. While older monuments occasionally include Ladino, it is much rarer than Yiddish.

Appliqué or Glue-on Lettering
The following photo gives a clear-cut reason why appliqué or glue-on lettering should be avoided. Notice that many letters are missing and the monument is less than 20-years old.

Beth David Memorial Gardens, Hollywood, FL

Section 1, Chapter 5. Decorations and Art on Monuments

The standard monument carvings are shown in many of the examples in this book.   This section gives some options that go well beyond the standard carvings:

Scenes
Modern technology allows for multi-colored scenes to be placed on tombstones. The theme below is a skiing scene but other monuments will show scenery of all sorts. As a caution: long term direct sunlight does fade most of the dyes used.

Tifferet Israel of Revere, Everett, MA

The Tree

United Jewish Brotherhood, Minneapolis

A cut off tree, a broken column or a stump are all used to indicate the person died before his/her time.

It is used most often for an unmarried individual who died, or in this case, was killed in battle, between age 10 and 25.

When it is on the grave of some-one older, it is usually because the selector of the monument liked the form but ignored the symbolism.

Occasionally, this symbol is on the grave of a younger child. Judaism is obsessed with life and living and as such, a fancy monument of this nature may be interpreted as putting too much emotional energy into a child that was non-viable.

Angels

The angel shown next from 2-angles is a beautiful piece of sculpture, although as suggested in the above entry on "trees", it is a bit over-the-top for a 2-year-old.

Minneapolis Hebrew, Minneapolis, MN

Cast Bronze

Decorations can be simple or complicated. On the left below is an eternal flame done simply and on the right is a bronze eternal flame which is turned into museum quality art.

United Jewish Brotherhood, Minneapolis, MN

41

Jewish Star

Similar to the eternal flame above, a Jewish Star (or *Magen David*) can be simple or complicated. On the left below is one done simply and on the right is museum quality art.

Colma, CA

Cameo Photos

A cameo photograph of the deceased became common as photographic technology became available. Many places no longer allow them. The fact that they are so common is indicative that the rabbinic community does not consider them to be in violation of the commandment banning "graven images." Even if cameo photos are allowed, my recommendation is not to use them. A disproportionate number of these are faded, stolen or vandalized. Below is a typical photograph of a grouping of monuments with vandalized or missing cameo photos from Woburn, MA.

If despite this warning, you choose to use a cameo photo, you may want to consider the following variation:

The frame with the cover protects the photo from fading caused by sunlight and also makes it immune to the casual vandal. Naturally, it is no protection against the committed vandal. These occur both in the "swing away" style shown below or with a "lift-up" hinge.

Lincoln Park Cemetery, *Chesed Shel Emet*, Warwick, RI

Section 1, Chapter 6. Children's Monuments

In an earlier time, children's graves were often placed along an edge of the cemetery. If there are monuments at all, they tend to be small. As cemeteries fill in, the separation between the children's section and the regular sections of cemeteries have all but disappeared. As of the early 21st century, children's monuments in most cemeteries are completely integrated into the main part of the cemeteries.

Jewish custom holds that one is not required to mourn a child who survives less than thirty days. Such a child is categorized with an unborn fetus. Cemetery sections for newborns and stillborns are sometimes referred to as a "*ne-fi-la*" (נפילא – Aramaic), the meaning "an untimely birth." The specific usage as "a lot to be set aside for untimely births" can be found in the Babylonian Talmud (Baba Batra 101b). Occasionally, there are monuments in the newborn/stillborn section, but usually not.

In today's world, this may seem harsh. But in the ancient world, childbirth and stillbirth were sufficiently common that the Jewish tradition emphasized getting on with life and living. By the late twentieth century, the frequency of pregnancy and the percentage of pregnancies that do not end in a viable birth had both decreased. As a result, each pregnancy has a greater importance in the life of the family. Responding to the needs and sensitivities of this era, the Reform rabbinate has added ceremonies for miscarriages and stillbirths.

All that being said, the most common children's markers tend to be small. An example is shown next.

Adath Israel, Massena, NY

Translation of Hebrew text:
Here lies
The lad, Nathan son of Dov Brennglass
Died on the 7th day of Passover 5740 (April 29, 1940)
Let his soul be bound up in the bonds of the living

If there is more than just name, date and standard iconography, the most common themes for children's graves are the broken tree, the angel and the lamb.

The broken tree is symbolic of a life "cut-off before its time." An example of this motif is shown in "Section 1, Chapter 5. Decorations and Art on Monuments."

An illustration of a child's monument incorporating an angel is shown in Section 1, Chapter 5. Decorations and Art on Monuments. A discussion of the pros and cons of the angel motif may be found in "Section 2, Chapter 5. In a Jewish Cemetery?"

The Lamb

The lamb has the symbolism of innocence. An example is shown next. It can either be a sculpture or an engraving.

Beech Street Cemeteries, Manchester, NH

Section 1, Chapter 7, Cenotaphs (Monuments for those buried elsewhere.)

For many, a cemetery is a place to visit and remember those who have passed away. And for some, it doesn't matter whether the remains of the person are there or not. There are many different reasons for cenotaphs as will be described in this chapter.

The most obvious cenotaphs are mass monuments for the deceased of wars and for those murdered by the Nazis in the Holocaust. These types of monuments tend to be commissioned works paid for and designed by a community and are not included for further discussion in this book. This chapter is about cenotaphs for an individual whose name is specifically mentioned.

Person Memorialized is buried Somewhere Else
Two examples are shown here. One is that of Isaac Touro who passed away in 1784 and is buried in Jamaica. After his death, his wife returned to Newport, RI. The family, who was centered in Newport, chose the cenotaph motif rather than a disinterment/re-interment, which is always problematic from an Orthodox Jewish point of view.

Example 1: Isaac Touro
The monument is a marble obelisk, a small piece of which is shown below. The east side is the monument to Reyna (Hays) Touro. The other three sides are a cenotaph to her husband, Isaac. The full inscription on the monument is shown next[7]: A few blanks shown on the west side are places where the monument is unreadable.

---

[7] Op. cit.: *The Old Jewish Cemetery of Newport...*, NH ©2007 pp. 93ff

South

West

Your dead men shall live,   יחיו מתיך נבלתי יקומון
together with my dead body
they shall arise. (Isaiah 16:19)

Monument   מצבת

for the memory of the learned   לזכרון המשכיל

honored and exalted _____   _____ הנכבד והגביר

Isaac, son of Abraham   יצחק בן אברהם טורא ז"ל

Touro of blessed memory.

reader and faithful   דק"ק ישועת ישראל _____ _____

pastor of the Holy Congregation
of Yeshuath Israel

50

who was released   נ"ל"ע ונקבר בקינגסתן יהמיקא
  for paradise and is buried in
  Kingston, Jamaica
  14 Tevet 5544   יי"ד טבת תקמ"ד לפ'ק

All the   ויהיו כל ימי שני חייו ששה וארבעים שנה

  days of the years of his life were 64 years.

Let his soul be bound up in the bonds of the living.   תנצב"ה'

North

Inscription
In memory of
the
Rev[d]. Isaac Touro
The able and faithful Minister
of the Congregation
Yeshuath Israel,
in New Port R.I.,
who departed this life
on the 14 Tebet A.M. 5544
and December 8, MDCCLXXXIII
at Kingston, Jamaica
where his remains lie buried
AE 46 years
the memory of the Just
is blessed.

East

Inscription
This tribute of
filial piety is consecrated
to the memory
of his honoured parents
by their son
ABRAHAM TOURO
MDCCCXIV

Example 2: Rita Abrams

Next, we have, Rita Abrams. While many non-Orthodox Jewish cemeteries allow for the burial of non-Jewish spouses, this cemetery does not. It is possible that her marriage to Bennett was a second marriage and she is buried by her first husband or it is possible that she was buried elsewhere because she was ineligible to be buried there.

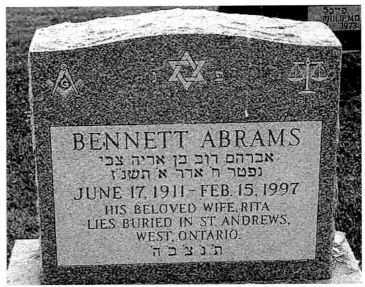

BENNETT ABRAMS

אברהם דוב בן אריה צבי
נפטר ח' אדר א' תשנ'ז

JUNE 17, 1911 - FEB. 15, 1997
HIS BELOVED WIFE, RITA
LIES BURIED IN ST. ANDREWS,
WEST, ONTARIO.
ת נ צ ב ה

Adath Israel, Massena, NY

A Disaffected Child

Because of the sensitivity involved, a situation is described that is true, but I will not give the name or location. I imagine the story is not unique, but one has to be an insider to know for sure.

Here is the story: A young lady who was born and raised as a Jew became very disaffected both by her family and by Judaism. Eventually, she married out and formally converted to Christianity. She died young and was buried

52

in a non-Jewish cemetery. Her parents had a monument placed for her in their family plot. There is nothing on the monument to indicate that she is not buried there.

Military
There are many cases in World War I and II, where individuals were buried in far away places, where a cenotaph was placed in their hometown cemetery.

Holocaust
Many cemeteries have what amounts to a *Yahrzeit* Board (a place where brass plaques are mounted in columns) listing the names of those whose graves are unknown and in many cases whose dates of death are also unknown.

Sometimes, the names are included at the bottom of tombstones as done in the following example. (Note that his wife had no problem with publishing the photo that follows, but asked that its location not be given.)

Recently, similar types of monuments have been added for victims of terror, but these are usually in addition to a more conventional monument.

פ"נ יקירנו
יצחק (איז'ו)
בן אפרים טאפט
ה' מרחשון התשס"ה

MICHAEL I.
TAFFET

SEPT. 7, 1923
OCT. 20, 2004
BELOVED   TENDER
RESOLUTE   BRAVE
HOLOCAUST SURVIVOR

לזכר אפרים דורה דבורקה
שייע מיצ'ו הניה ופיני
אשר נספו בשואה

Just below where it says "Holocaust Survivor", the inscription reads:

In memory of Efraim, Dora, Deborah,
Shia,Mitzi, Haniah and Pini
who were wiped out in the Holocaust.

Lost at Sea

The memorial that follows is for sailors lost at sea when an Israeli submarine disappeared. The layout of the monuments, if one did a "connect-the-dots" looking at it from the air, is designed to looks like a submarine.

Mt. Herzl, Jerusalem, Israel

Section 1, Chapter 8: Mausoleums and Niches

A mausoleum is a large tomb or a building housing a tomb or several tombs, where the coffin containing the body is placed in an above-ground vault. There are Jewish monuments that to the casual observer may appear to be mausoleums. The difference is that in a mausoleum, the body is stored in an above-ground vault. An *O-hel* or *Nefesh* in Hebrew or *Hoisl* in Yiddish is often a shrine at the burial sites of famous Jews, usually rabbis. In these burial sites, the body is underground beneath the structure. Several examples of these are shown in Section 2.

There are no formal Jewish traditions that apply to mausoleums or to niches/columbariums. Jewish burial custom requires that the body be returned to the ground. Therefore these types of tombs are not historically approved by any major branch of Judaism. However, they exist in some Jewish cemeteries in all major metropolitan areas.

When an entombment occurs, the panel at the end of the vault is removed and the coffin is slid in. The granite panel covering is sent to the monument maker who adds the inscription and then returns the panel to be replaced. This is an example of a vault with a covering missing.

Beth David Memorial Gardens, Hollywood, FL

Also available are spaces that are oriented toward the length of the body. They require more than double the width and more finished surface area. They are therefore more expensive.

Mausoleums

Mausoleums range from large buildings built by cemetery associations that include the remains of many, unrelated individuals or to small structures containing the remains of one person or related family members. Below, gives an overview of just how big one of these public mausoleums can be.

Beth David Memorial Gardens, Hollywood, FL

Individual vaults are usually covered by a slab of granite which may be inscribed with pretty much anything the deceased or his/her survivors wanted, space permitting. The inscriptions may be traditional or not.

The Mann monument is a reasonably traditional monument inscription with one of the standard Jewish icons, namely the candelabra. While there tends to be less Hebrew, you can find fully traditional Hebrew inscriptions.

Beth David Memorial Gardens, Hollywood, FL

Next, we have a non-traditional inscription which gives the reader a little insight into what must have been a humorous personality.

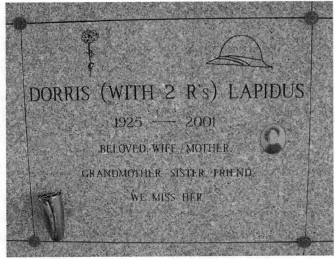

Beth David Memorial Gardens, Hollywood, FL

Costs for these vary depending on whether they are at ground level, heart-level, eye-level or higher. Higher vaults are less expensive. Ground-level, heart-level and eye-level are at a premium. As of ca. 2010, typical prices for these for the higher vaults are about three to five times more expensive than a conventional burial plot. Ground level and heart-level and eye-level are typically four to eight times more costly than a conventional burial plot. These prices vary from city-to-city are given only for guidance purposes.

Private Mausoleums
Some families design their own private mausoleums or have them designed. In addition, there are companies that have catalogs for private mausoleums. The price can range from about $100,000 in ca. 2010 prices and go up into the millions.

A modest private mausoleum is shown below.

Beth David Memorial Gardens, Hollywood, FL

An opulent one is shown next.

Colma Complex, CA

Niches or Columbariums

Niches or columbariums are places where urns with cremains (cremation remains) are placed. They are inscribed in much the same way as mausoleums are. Note that Judaism does not formally approve of cremation, but there are individual rabbis who find them acceptable. *Section 3: Chapter 1. Where Reality and the Theoretical Diverge* briefly describes the problem with cremation.

Niches tend to be about one square foot and cost about the same as a conventional burial plot.

A few examples are shown next. Note that there is room for inscriptions, icons, and a vase for a floral arrangement. Some-times, the inscription is on a brass plaque. The ones shown were likely sandblasted.

Beth David Memorial Gardens, Hollywood, FL

In the above example, the containers for the remains are behind a granite panel. In the next example, the urns are displayed behind glass

Colma, CA

In summary, mausoleums and niche/columbariums do exist in some Jewish cemeteries. This is apparently based on a measure of assimilation to non-Jewish American burial customs. This chapter is not intended to be an endorsement for this choice.

Section 1, Chapter 9. Pebbles, Pebbles and More Pebbles

Most of the time, when I give lectures on cemeteries, one question I am consistently asked is, "Why do you Jews put pebbles on tombstones?" There are few questions of Jewish custom that do not have more than one answer and the pebble question is no exception. Dr. Mareleyn Schneider has written an article that includes 37-different plausible answers to that question[8]!

A short answer and the most popular answer follows: Judaism teaches that the guarantee of immortality to the deceased is how the dead are remembered by the living. Pebbles on a monument show other visitors that the individual buried on that site has been visited recently and has not been forgotten.

As recently as the 1996 printing of *The Jewish Mourner's Book of Why*, Alfred Kolatch states[9], "Reform Jews do not, as a rule, leave reminders on tombstones" and he bases that on some mid-70's writings of Rabbi Solomon Freehof. While this may been true when Freehof wrote it, this is certainly not true today!

The use of pebbles has not only become ubiquitous among Jewish cemetery visitors, it is starting to show up in non-Jewish cemeteries. Shown next is a monument in a non-Jewish cemetery complete with a Celtic Cross and pebbles!

---

[8] "Why Jews Place Pebbles or Rocks on Tombstones", by Mareleyn Schneider, Ph.D., Yeshiva University, 2007. First published as Appendix G. in the Third Printing and later editions of *A Field Guide to Visiting a Jewish Cemetery*, by Rabbi Joshua Segal, ©2005, JCP, LLC, NH

[9] *The Jewish Mourner's Book of Why*, by Alfred Kolatch, Jonathan David, NY, copyright 1993, page 232

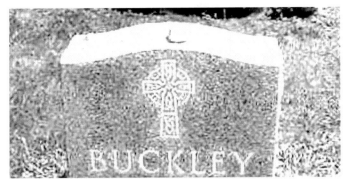

North Cemetery, Wayland, MA

Note that many cemeteries make "visitation stones" or "remembrance stones" available as they are called in the two photos below. The first photo is a container holding pebbles for visitors to which they can help themselves and use.

Bet Olam, Wayland, MA

By contrast, in our "artificial world," Norbeck Memorial Park combines the need of visitors to place stones/pebbles with practical consideration of their lawn maintenance equipment, by making "wooden disks" available:

Norbeck Memorial Park, Olney, MD

- - - - -

Shrines
Once the tradition of leaving "stuff" on tombstones became normative, everything that one could imagine to be left – is left!

Roadside make-shift shrines have been popping up where people die in car accidents. Similar shrines are surrounding tombstones both in Jewish and non-Jewish cemeteries, especially of young people.

The monument shown next has pebbles, shells, toys and *chach-kas* (knick-knacks) of all sorts on it. The top of the

67

photo is a close up of the top-right of the monument shown below it.

Bet Olam, Wayland

Carved Objects

It seems as an industry is developing around monuments with small carved stones and cast pieces being used as "calling cards." Grandchildren are leaving painted rocks and shown below is even a casting a paw print of a pet!

All of the above photographed at Bet Olam, Wayland, MA

Sports

Anyone who lived in the Boston area who was a Red Sox fan knew the pain of the "Babe Ruth curse." Many lived their lives between 1918 and 2004 never seeing their Sox as World Champions. Consistent with "pebble-style-ephemera", many tombstones have decoration as follows immediately after the Red Sox 2004 victory and their repeat in 2007,

Linwood, Randolph, MA

Oskar Schindler

Sometimes the stone can be so covered with pebbles, that it is almost difficult to see the monument! Due to the movie, *Schindler's List,* most people are familiar with the name, Oskar Schindler. Schindler, a non-Jew, is buried in the Christian cemetery on Mt. Zion in Jerusalem. To demonstrate both the magnitude and breadth of pebble usage, his gravesite and monument are shown next:

Mt. Zion, Jerusalem, Israel

Section 1, Chapter 10. Perpetual Care (or Perpetual Neglect)

The concept of perpetual care for cemetery plots is relatively new. It used to be the family's responsibility to take care of burial plots. The net result was gross neglect of cemeteries, especially older ones. Recognizing this problem, most cemeteries sell plots that include "perpetual care." While there are some cemeteries that do reasonably well with it, in the vast majority of cases, the only guarantee for perpetual care is that the grass will be cut. They don't repair broken stones, straighten crooked ones, clean lichens, clean bird droppings, etc.

If maintenance/preservation gets done at all, it is through the good will of some volunteer organization. The real problem is, that if the volunteer organization doesn't know what they are doing, they can cause short term good, but a longer term damage. What follows are some examples of "perpetual neglect."

Some of the problems shown in this chapter can be planned for proactively. Others put us at the mercy of the good will of those who follow us to fix or maintain gravesites.

Recognizing the maintenance problem, many newer cemeteries have strict policies for monument size and materials.

Tire Treads

The tread marks on the monument below show clearly that the lawn mowing crew was more concerned with getting a job done than respecting the burial site.

Temple Beth Abraham, Nashua, NH

Shrubs

Shrubs need to be trimmed. The monument below shows, that even if they are trimmed occasionally, the shrubs aren't trimmed often enough.

Temple Beth Abraham, Nashua, NH

In extreme cases, as shown next, you will see monuments ejected from the ground or tipped over by root growth. While the tree is dead and cut, repairing the root damage would be difficult.

Minneapolis Hebrew, Minneapolis, MN

Scuffed stone
Notice how the bottom of the monument is scarred by repeated near approaches by weed-whackers or other lawn care equipment.

Stone covered by clippings

The next shows what I would characterize as the disappearance of ground level monuments typical of memorial parks of today. The stone settles and after a few years of clippings, the stone slowly disappears. For these reasons, I strongly discourage surface flat monuments, although some cemeteries require them.

Adath Israel, Massena, NY

Section 2:
Funny, Peculiar, and Unique: A Ceoss-section from the Serious to Humorous in Cemeteries

In designing a monument, one must ask the questions: For whom is the monument intended? Is it for the deceased? Is it for the immediate family and friends? Or is it for posterity and for any passerby? Or perhaps, it is for all of the above.

If it is only for the deceased, there is no need for either a monument or inscription. The deceased will never get to read it. If it is for the immediate family and friends, then the monument could and should provide a message that will be meaningful to them. If it is for posterity and any passerby, then some care must be taken to understand how the inscription will be perceived.

In addition, there are the situations over which we have no control or "the law of unintended consequences." The following monument shown is from a non-Jewish cemetery in Georgetown, DC, and it is an example where the juxtaposition of two nearby inscriptions can transform two serious inscriptions into something of humor.

The monument is an obelisk, very common in mid-19th century American cemeteries.

On the right side of the obelisk, the inscription reads: "... died after a short and painful illness... 1866 ..."

75

The full inscription, not clear in the photo, reads:

SACRED
to the memory of
FRANCIS N. HOLTZMAN
who departed this life
after a short and painful illness
August 25th 1866
in the 29th year of his age

While this is sad, it certainly is not funny. However, when one looks at the other side of the monument, it appears that Mr. Holtzman's father had passed away some 29-years earlier. He is memorialized on the left side of the very same monument.

The inscription reads: "... died after a long and painful illness ... 1837."

The full inscription, also not clear in the photo, reads:

SACRED
to the memory of
JOHN HOLTZMAN
who departed this life
after a long and painful illness
Nov. 20th 1837
in the 45th year of his age

While there is nothing necessarily funny about the pain of either Mr. Holtzman, the juxtaposition of the two inscriptions tickled me!

The remainder of this section is intended to show:
1. serious inscriptions and iconography
2. serious inscriptions and iconography that can be interpreted as humorous
3. inscriptions and iconography clearly intended as humorous from the start

There are also examples of the misinterpretations caused by generational differences in our understanding of language; of the disasters caused by poor editing; and of the effect of coincidence when the placement of one inscription of monument, juxtaposed with another, creates an odd situation.

Section 2, Chapter 1. A Few Words that say a Lot

Our collective understanding of certain phrases, allows us to say a lot in a few words. In the monument below, with the first two words of Proverbs 31:10ff, *Ei-shet cha-yil* (A woman of Valor – אשת חיל), the message is, "this is the perfect wife." That is, to anyone who is familiar with this passage!

Temple Beth Abraham, Nashua, NH

- - - - -

Some have said that women are about relationships and men are about careers.

On the right side of the monument below, one doesn't even need to know the context of Song of Songs 5:16 (THIS IS MY BELOVED...) to recognize that this man was more than the perfunctory beloved of ELAINE, named in line 4 of the inscription. As such, it follows, that the decoration (i.e. the ring) on her side could be understood as a wedding ring, with the circle being a perfect shape with no beginning and no end. But what about the monkey wrench on his side? Perhaps he was a plumber, although this doesn't

79

make most of the published lists of accepted monument symbolism.

But what does the inscription, "SHE REALLY TRIED" mean? That's not from any source that I recognize.

Bnai Brith, Peabody, MA

Zebras and doctors

Sometimes, a particular expression which appears on a gravestone is not from the Bible or traditional sources. It may be a private joke, a community expression, or, as in the following example, professional jargon or a running professional in-joke.

Town of Wayland's North Cemetery, MA

Translation	Transcription of Inscription
Just because you hear the	(sic דהירה) כשתשמע קול דחירת
sound of hoof beats	
don't expect	(sic תצפה) אל תצפות
to see a zebra.	(sic זברה) לראות זברח

When I first saw the inscription above, I searched the Talmud and other Jewish sources, to no avail. Then I happened to speak about it to a member of the medical profession, who explained to me that it is a common expression among physicians. "If you hear hoof beats, expect horses, not zebras" usually means "don't look for an extra-ordinary solution until the standard ones have been exhausted."

While it is common to translate Hebrew texts into English, this inscription is unusual in that it translates a common English expression into Hebrew. But independent of that, what message is being given?

Was this just an expression that the deceased physician used routinely, so his survivors placed it as a reminder of these words of wisdom? Was there some measure of irony in that the doctor passed away from something obscure because they looked at the simple, or vice verse? Or was it something completely different?

Section 2, Chapter 2. Puns, Play on Words, Double Entendres and Nicknames

The Salloways were apparently strongly into music. The clarinet on the left and the measure of music on the right are certainly eye catching. But the base of the stone contains the line, "HARMONY 1 BROUGHT US TOGETHER" which is a lovely sentiment (and pun) not only on music, but on their lives together.

Maple Hill, Peabody, MA

- - - - -

In the next example, the fishing pole is punned with the epitaph, "TOP OF THE LINE."

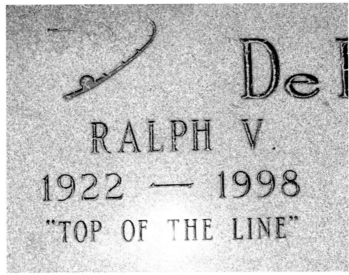

Star of David, Fort Lauderdale, FL

- - - - -

Nicknames can be telling. The word, "buff" has one risqué meaning associated with nudity, although the word also has many other meanings. In the monument that follows, what does "BUFF" mean? Is it just a nickname or is it some insider joke?

Menorah Garden, Fort Lauderdale, FL

- - - - -

The monument shown below also appears later in Chapter 3, titled, "Popular Culture and Logos": "Bubba" means grandma in Yiddish, but it is not usually spelled this way[10]. In the mid-1990's, when this monument was made, that specific spelling had a redneck implication associated with it. Again the question arises: just a nickname or some insider joke?

Montifiore, Woburn, MA

- - - - -

And what do we want to infer about Mr. Perfect?

Mt. Nebo, Miami, FL

- - - - -

---

[10] More common is "Bubbie", "Baubie" or "Bubbe."

And if Mr. Perfect weren't difficult enough, what do you suppose "beloved wife and mother Nancy" did to become Mrs. Satan?

Mt. Nebo, Miami, FL

- - - - -

For Jack Del Rio, the "Jack of Our Hearts" takes us to a deck of cards. Note the reference to "Knight" and remember that some of the Jacks were knights.[11] Also unusual is that the epitaph is actually signed by someone, namely, "Susan."

Menorah Garden, Fort Lauderdale, FL

- - - - -

---

[11] Jack of Spades: Ogier the Dane – Jack of Hearts: La Hire – Jack of Diamonds: Hector – Jack of Clubs: Lancelot

The following isn't a pun or a nickname, but it's a clever use of the number sequence: 8, 1 and zero (also a rhyme: one and none):

SIDNEY KRAKAUER
שעיה בן יעקב
DECEMBER 13, 1919 — OCTOBER 30, 1989
חשון 2 5750
FATHER OF EIGHT
HUSBAND OF ONE
SECOND TO NONE

Star of David, Fort Lauderdale, FL

Section 2, Chapter 3. Popular Culture and Logos

Popular culture and logos become part of people's lives and are reflected in the following examples.

Diamond Lil

Diamond Lil is a 1928 play by American actress and playwright Mae West. Diamond Lil was about a racy woman in the 1890s. She was also a Marvel cartoon super-hero.

It is unlikely the author of the tombstone was branding the woman in a negative light, as can be seen from the choice of "She was a woman of Valor (Proverbs 31)" a Biblical description of the perfect wife. But it is probably intended as a loving comment about a woman who liked her jewelry. Note also, the affectation of dotting the "I" with a "heart."

Evergreen, Fort Lauderdale, FL

The Greatest

The following may or may not have been based on Mohammed Ali's boast. Or it could also have been based on Jackie Gleason's use of the same line in the "Honeymooners." As a passerby and given the colloquial, those are the images that come to me. It points to a dangerous phenomenon: what happens when the meaning of language changes and the classical intent of what is written changes?

Mohammed Ali stated, "I am the greatest" and I suspect that all of us want to think of ourselves that way. Helen or her survivors didn't have it cast in concrete, but she (or they) did have it cast in bronze!

Menorah Garden, Fort Lauderdale, FL

Munchkin

The word *"munchkin"* came into the English language through a dwarflike race portrayed in L. Frank Baum's "The Wonderful Wizard of Oz" (1900) and popularized in the 1939 movie, "The Wizard of Oz." It has further been trademarked by Dunkin Donuts for a donut hole served as a mini-donut. So was Stacy small, was she a donut lover, or something else? Regardless, it is a charming reference to someone who died at such a young age (22).

Maple Hill, Peabody, MA

90

The Three Stooges
As with many of the popular culture monuments shown,
the possibilities for what is meant here is anybody's guess!

Beech Street Cemeteries, Manchester, NH

Logos
On the monument of a 93 year old woman who died in
1994 is the name, Eva "Bubba" Wiseman. The monument
is shown below.

Her date of birth and death were inscribed on the bottom.
Her Hebrew name and Hebrew date of death are at the top.
In the upper left corner is a floral pattern and between her
common calendar day of birth and death is a candelabrum.
On her "name line" we have Eva "Bubba" means grandma
in Yiddish and was discussed in the chapter titled, "Puns,
Play on Words and Double Entendres"

But in the upper right hand corner, shown in a blow-up
next to the monument, is a beer can with the word
"Budweiser" inscribed on it. Maybe this was a pun: Bubba

Wiseman = Bud Weiser? Was the family reflecting on some aspect of her life that gave her joy, namely: beer? Maybe beer became a humorous footnote to her life in her dotage.

Montifiore, Woburn, MA

- - - - -

Below, we see the monument of George Weinstein, born in 1890. Cards are fairly common and several examples are shown in a later chapter. But he ups the ante from the "Budweiser can" above to a whiskey glass!

Emanu El, San Bernardino, CA

And, it appears that George would have been 25 when Lester was born. So I infer that George was Lester's father. Lester, whose monument is shown below, was the acorn who didn't fall far from the tree.

The cards: Father – Blackjack: Son – Poker
The liquor: Father – generic glass: Son – Jack Daniels
The center: Father – cigars: Son – the theater

Emanu El, San Bernardino, CA

- - - - -

One of the great American status symbols was the Cadillac. For the Jew of the mid-20th century, driving a Cadillac was the emblem that one had made it. As a matter of fact, the Cadillac, known for its very smooth ride, was often referred to as a "boat" and in the anti-Semitic world, the Cadillac was known as a "Jew Canoe."

Regardless of the reason, the monument below includes the Cadillac logo.

Star of David, Fort Lauderdale, FL

- - - - -

The following logo has a certain "air" about it, namely, Chanel No. 5 on the left. And all of the reputed love that Jews have for Chinese food comes together in the fortune cookie below on the right.

United Jewish Brotherhood, Minneapolis, MN

Section 2, Chapter 4. Cards and Card Playing

Cards and card playing has been popular among Jews. Many of the greatest contract bridge players, Goren, Scheinwold, Kaplan, Fishbein, etc. were if not Jewish, of Jewish descent. As poker has become popular, it seems that many names on the tournaments broadcast on television give someone aware of characteristically Jewish names, the idea a disproportionately high fraction of high level poker players are Jewish.

The following entry shows just a "Joker." This could be either a nickname or a card player.

Menorah Gardens, Fort Lauderdale

- - - - -

Next we have the perfect seven-no-trump bridge hand:

Palm Springs, CA

- - - - -

And, on a monument that we saw in an earlier chapter, we have the Royal Flush in spades, the perfect poker hand.

Emanu El, San Bernardino, CA

- - - - -

And not to be outdone, we have the perfect Blackjack hand, although with the ace-ten combination, it might also have been pinochle.

Emanu El, San Bernardino, CA

- - - - -

In the final example, with two hands, it's not clear what game is being shown, although the King-Queen on the left could be husband-wife or part of a pinochle meld. Note that the right hand is on the left and the left hand is on the right!

Palm Springs, CA

Section 2, Chapter 5. In a Jewish Cemetery?

There are logical reasons that non-Jewish motifs find their way into Jewish cemeteries. Among the reasons are both errors and ignorance. But sometimes, it is intentional oversight. For example, in times of grief, if something provides comfort to a family, occasionally the community will look the other way. Also, sometimes a person who is very wealthy or who has wealthy survivors will ask for something that is Jewishly inappropriate in exchange for a large donation or in consideration for previous donations. Communities will sometimes yield to that kind of financial pressure. Exceptions also occur because in some cemeteries, no one reviews or censors the contents of monuments. This may explain why so many monuments have mistakes both in grammar and in content. However, a major purpose of cemeteries and monuments is to provide comfort to the family and friends of the deceased. With that in mind, visitors will continue to encounter the things that follow.

- - - - -

One can't prevent a guest from placing things on or around a monument. And before the caretaker has a chance to clean it up, someone, such as me, comes along and takes a photograph. But the following in a Jewish cemetery push the envelope:

The "Christian Guardian Angel" when it does appear, usually appears on a child's grave. Below is on an older adult grave. Jewishly speaking, there is nothing inherently wrong with angels. However, based on medieval art as well as modern lawn displays and shrines, there are specific angel motifs that are "generally understood to be Christian." In asserting Jewish identity, imitation of non-Jewish practice, called, *Chu-kat Ha-go-yim* is prohibited.

Star of David, Fort Lauderdale, FL

And while the Christmas poinsettias below are surprising, in another cemetery in San Francisco's Colma complex, there was a monument (not shown here) where the poinsettias had a Santa Claus ornament hanging from the floral arrangement!

Palm Springs, CA

Who is Editing the Content?
While the decorations may be surprising, sometimes, what is actually inscribed on the tombstone makes one wonder: Who is checking before the monuments are inscribed?

<u>Namaste or Praying Hands</u>
To the casual observer, the "namaste" or "praying hands" are interchangeable in appearance. The namaste is a greeting used by Hindus, Jains and Buddhists, understood to mean, that "I respect that divinity within you that is also within me." It has become especially popular in the 21st century used in the context of yoga.

Its symbolism as "praying hands" is Christian. But whether it is a "namaste" or "praying hands", the use of Hindu, Jain, Buddhist or Christian symbols in a Jewish cemetery, while not funny, is certainly odd or unusual.

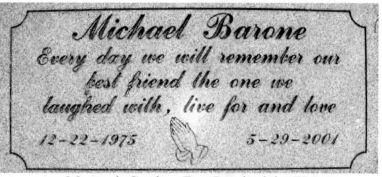

Menorah Garden, Fort Lauderdale, FL

- - - - -

Kneeling?

The inscription that follows on the tombstone of a child includes a kneeling child with a fairly common Christian prayer. Jews don't kneel in prayer and a more appropriate selection might have been the *She-ma* (Deut. 6:4), a prayer asserting God's unity. That prayer, which is often recited at bedtime, frequently appears on Jewish tombstones.

Mt. Nebo, Miami, FL

- - - - -

Religious Overtones in Word Choice

It is very likely that Irving, memorialized in the next monument, regularly used the expression, "JEEZ, WHAT A DEAL". The censors obviously missed that "JEEZ" is a euphemism for Jesus that is often used as a euphemism in the Christian world to avoid taking the name of their Lord in vain.

Star of David, Fort Lauderdale, FL

- - - - -

Non-Jews in a Jewish Cemetery

Many Jewish cemeteries do not allow burials of non-Jews. As mixed marriage has continued to grow, some Jewish cemeteries will allow non-Jewish burials or have a special section for these couples. However, there is usually a restriction in the cemetery's bylaws that states: No non-Jewish religious symbols are permitted on stones of non-Jewish spouses.

Below is a part of a stone of a non-Jew. Since his wife was Jewish, he was eligible for burial in this cemetery. The inscription "Blessed by God at 423 Main Street, Erie, PA on July 13th 1896" was a sneaky way to get around the rules. This was apparently the address at which this man was baptized on the listed date in 1896! Note also, the tree at the top seems to makes the trunk and branches look like a cross. Details of who and where, as well as the complete photo of the stone are intentionally omitted.

BLESSED BY GOD
JULY 13TH 1896
509 EAST 26TH ST.
ERIE, PENNSYLVANIA.

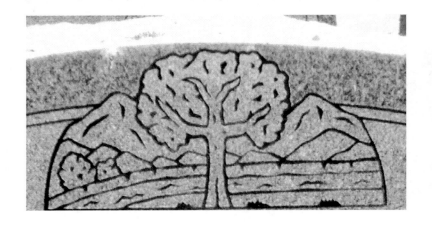

A Cross?

The Fleur-de-Lis, shown below in the upper left, is sometimes used as a cross. When it appears in Jewish cemeteries, it is almost always as the logo for "The Boy Scouts."

B'nai Brith Lodge Cemetery, Worcester, MA

Non-Jewish Theology #1

The monument shown to the right expresses an idea that is commonly held in some faith communities, but certainly not Judaism. To suggest that God took away someone's beloved because "God needed him/her more" implies a God who is mean spirited and by extension, unworthy of our worship.

United Jewish Brotherhood, Minneapolis, MN

Non-Jewish Theology #2
The epitaph of a woman named Rose reads:
"G-D NEEDED ANOTHER ROSE
TO COMPLETE HIS BOUQUET"

Elmwood Complex, Troy, NY

As with the first example, to suggest that God took away someone's beloved because "God needed her to complete a bouquet," implies a God who is superficial and by extension, unworthy of our worship.

Section 2, Chapter 6. Song Lyrics

Songs and music are period pieces which reflect a period in time and create very visceral reactions. With the exception of the classics, it's probably why most of us love the music of our formative years, but hate the music of our parents and our children. What follow are a number of examples where the epitaph is either the title of a popular song or the lyrics from one.

To Know Him Was to Love Him
For Irving Levine, "To know him was to love him." This 1958 song by the Teddy Bears was #1 on Billboard's Top Rock and Roll hits.

Menorah Garden, Fort Lauderdale, FL

My Way
For Irving Simon, the epitaph is "You better do it my (i.e. his) way." This was of course, a Parody on Frank Sinatra's 1969 song, "My Way". Note that Frank Sinatra was a resident of Palm Springs and although not Jewish, Sinatra was both a supporter of Israel and the Palm Springs synagogue.

Palm Springs, CA

On the Road Again
Stuart Kaplan must have liked to travel, given that his epitaph is the title of the hit song performed by Willie Nelson, Bob Dylan and others. Due to the overlap of the Kaplan's life with the various performers associated with the song, it's less clear with which of the artists he is identifying with.

Palm Springs, CA

Enjoy Yourself...
Enjoy Yourself, It's Later Than You Think, by Carl Sigman and Herb Magidson, was written in 1948. The song has been recorded many times by diverse artists such as Bing Crosby, Tommy Dorsey, Guy Lombardo, Doris Day, etc.

As a message on Rosa's monument, the lyrics could have been a favorite song of hers or a lament of her survivors!

Bet Olam, Wayland, MA

Margie

"I'm always thinking of you, Margie" are lyrics from the song, *Margie*, lyrics written by Benny Davis and music by J. Russell Robinson and Con Conrad, 1920.

Only infrequently am I able to get the story behind a monument. This little footstone was very carefully planned and designed by Marjorie's daughter, Carol. She told me that the song was a favorite of Marjorie's mother, in particular a version with Eddie Cantor singing. The song probably influenced her choice about selecting Marjorie's name. In their home, the music was always out on their piano, but no one ever played it. At the unveiling, there was a member of the family who was an opera singer. They asked him if he would sing it, but he never heard the song before. The unveiling was a few days short of two years after Marjorie's death, which is an unusually long delay. Part of the delay of putting in the tombstone was that initially, there were those in the family who thought the inscription was "too cutesy". After the fact, everyone seems to agree that it is a most fitting memorial. As an aside, for those who actually read music and know the song, there is at least one minor error in the music as written.

Beth El, Paramus, NJ

109

Section 2, Chapter 7. "I'd rather be" and "the Passions of a Lifetime"

The mid-20th century comedian and actor, W. C. Fields was known to have found Philadelphia to be a difficult town in which to perform. There is no epitaph on his grave but it is a widely reported urban myth that his self-written epitaph reads, "I would rather be living in Philadelphia".

- - - - -

The epitaphs that follow are parodies of W. C. Fields' theoretical epitaph which let the reader know that the person buried here would much rather be alive:

We begin with Jack Greenberg would rather be golfing.

Palm Springs, CA

- - - - -

Leon Block shown next, would rather be flying. And decorations that include fishing gear, baseball bats and you name it, are indicative of the breadth of activities in which the deceased would prefer to be engaged!

Palm Springs, CA

- - - - -

The following are taken from four-different monuments in the United Jewish Brotherhood Cemetery, Minneapolis, MN. They include bowling pins, a football, a basketball and a tennis racket. Golf clubs, baseball bats, skis and almost anything else one could imagine, can also be found.

Irving the Unnerving

The vast majority of memorable inscriptions are just mini-views into someone's life and the viewers of those inscriptions need to allow their imagination to tell the story.

In Irving's case, I found his obituary[12] which indicated that Irving was a decorated Korean War vet who earned two bronze stars. "His patriotism was fervent, his defense of the Jewish people fiery." He was committed to the Jewish War Veterans (JWV), social welfare and his family.

In addition to the obituary, I also spoke to his daughter, Diane Nielson. She told me that the inscription on the monument that follows was written by Irving and left on Diane's sister's desk. I asked her, "For whom did she think the epitaph was intended?" She responded, "Initially for himself, then the family bought in – and after the fact, the eternal memory offered by its being noticed, enhances his life and legacy." She further said, that if anyone in the family or the cemetery objected to the inscription she was unaware of it

---

[12] "Taps for Irving Hauptman", by Jeanette Friedman, July 5, 2006
http://www.jstandard.com/index.php/content/item/1944/

Cedar Park Cemetery, Paramus, NJ

HERE LIES
IRVING THE UNNERVING
NO MORE VETERANS IS HE SERVING
THE LORD NOW HE IS OBSERVING
PATRIOTIC IRVING THE DESERVING
FOREVER IN OUR HEARTS

114

Section 2, Chapter 8. Errors

Once a mistake is made, there are a variety of methods by which it can be fixed. The following example shows that a NOV (November) date of birth was erroneously put on the monument and it was corrected to JAN (January). The mistake looks good at the time of the unveiling of the monument. However, the photo that follows shows that mistakes are usually "forever"! This photo was taken about after 25 years after the monument was erected. Wear and erosion took its toll.

Oops, missed a word!
Filling in a missed word on 18th century monuments is common. This 1972 monument once again emphasizes the importance of editing! To the credit of those involved, at least this monument was fixed! In most cases, errors are just left for eternity.

BELOVED SON
AND BROTHER
JOSEPH
ABELOW
FEB. 5, 1972
אחינו

Center Street, West Roxbury

God Repairs

The following story was related to me. The teller told me I could use it, as long as I didn't mention him by name.

> My late father-in-law was a very difficult person, to say the least. Never physically abusive, and having a low self-esteem, he was verbally abusive in ways that permanently scarred his wife and children.
>
> On a recent visit to the cemetery it was evident that providence is ever at work. Bird droppings on his monument had all but totally obliterated the word "beloved" from the inscription, "beloved husband and father."

Just as erosion exposes mistakes, a pigeon became God's agent to amend accordingly.

English Errors

Because it is harder to edit foreign language texts, i.e. Hebrew, we might forget that mistakes can also occur in English.

Below is the monument of Israel Pastor. The top of the photo is the front of the monument. The bottom photo is the back of the monument with Mr. Pastor's name spelled, "Isreal". While there are individuals who choose to spell their name that way, it is clear that when the name is spelled both ways on the same monument, that one of the two must be incorrect.

Temple Beth Abraham, Nashua, NH

- - - - -

Hebrew Errors

The following is an example where the omission of a single Hebrew letter (') surely changes the perspective! Note, that in the English part of the inscription, it does say, "Dear wife." The first line and translation are on the left. What I believe was intended is on the right!

Translation of the Error	Error	Intended translation	As intended
A frigid wife	אשה קרה	Beloved wife	אשה יקרה

Independent Gold Crown, Woburn, MA

The mistake in the Hebrew on the monument on the monument of a woman who died in 1937 that follows is somewhere between amusing and outrageous.

Crawford Street Shul, Baker St., W. Roxbury, MA

Translation of the Error	Error	Intended translation	As intended
my whore	זוֹנָתִי	my mate (or wife)	זוּגָתִי

The translation of the 1st Hebrew line as written is "My whore and our beloved mother." The translation of 1st Hebrew line as I suspect was intended is "My beloved wife and our beloved mother."

118

Section 2, Chapter 9. Names and Decorations

Sometimes, the name is descriptive of what we are looking at, namely, Stone's stone:

Adath Israel, Massena, NY

- - - - -

Here is one where the designation of "*ko-hein* (priest)" in the Hebrew, happens to be the translation of "*ko-hein*" in English.

B'nai Brith Lodge Cemetery, Worcester, MA

Popular in Europe are decorations where the decorations reflect the name of the deceased. For example, a person named "Hahn", Yiddish for "hen", might have a chicken on his or her stone. While not common in America, the stone that follows has a torch on it and Lapidos (לפידות) does translate as "torch".

Linwood, Randolph, MA

- - - - -

On the other hand, the use of a pitcher is common on tombstones of Levites.[13] What is unique about the pitcher below is that the pitcher actually spells out the Hebrew word, לוי, leaving no doubt that this is a Levitic pitcher and not a Beer pitcher.

Mt. Nebo, Miami, FL

- - - - -

Rose

Usually, the decoration, when associated with the name of the deceased, is associated with the surname. Here is an example where the decoration deals with the middle name, with Rose, being remembered with a rose.

Kopiagorod, Baker Street, West Roxbury, MA

---

[13] For those who claim to be direct descendants of Jacob's son, Levi, are called *le-vi-im*, לוים," the Levites." The pitcher as shown at the top of the monument is what they use to wash the hands of the priest when the Priestly Benediction (Nu. 6:24-26) is offered. *Le-vi-im* (Levites) are given vestigial honors within Orthodox and Conservative synagogues.

121

Unicorn

The unicorns on the top left and top right are a cute way of translating "Einhorn" (one horn) to "unicorn".

Beth Emeth, Albany, NY

- - - - -

Developmental Progression of Symbolism

The menorah or candelabrum appears on some women's monuments. The lighting of candles is a commandment (mitsvah) specifically designated for a woman to perform. Older monuments show these candelabras with two, three, four, five or seven branches.

Some newer monuments use a nine-branched Chanukah menorah (*Chanukiah*). This appears to be a morphing of the Shabbat candles, likely due to assimilation. As Shabbat candles became less important to some assimilated Jews, the *Chanukiah* became a

more meaningful symbol than Shabbat candles.

Mixed Symbols

There are many symbols that developed in Victorian cemeteries and some that are pretty much exclusively Jewish. Shown next are two examples of combining two symbols in a single decoration. The first combines two Jewish symbols, namely the Jewish Star (*Magen David*) and the menorah (candelabra). The second combines the Jewish Star with cut wheat. Wheat is symbolic of "the final harvest" or death, but the combination shows the way secular symbolism and in some cases non-Jewish symbolism, has found its way into Jewish cemeteries.

Both from Linwood, Randolph, MA

The shape of the monument?

So far, we've had examples of iconography matching the name of the deceased and the adaptation of Victorian symbolism into Jewish Cemeteries We may never know if this monument shape to the left was selected to reflect the shape of a candle (Kandel) or if it was selected by someone who just liked the obelisk shape.

Beth El, Paramus, NJ

Section 2, Chapter 10. Cause of Death

Many epitaphs include the cause of death. One of the most commonly reported epitaphs of this nature, both in Jewish and non-Jewish cemeteries is: "I told you I was sick." However it is clear from the number of monuments that include this information, that family and survivors feel the need to document the cause of death. What follows, are a few examples:

Lightning: (Congregation Ahavat Shalom, Lynn, No. Reading, MA)
Note that my translation attempted to maintain the poetry of the Hebrew; and the transliteration is included to demonstrate the rhyme and meter of the Hebrew inscription.

The lightning flashed,	*Hei-ir ba-rak*	האיר ברק
thunder did roar,	*Nish-ma ra-am*	נשמע רעם
and the heart ,	*ve-leiv*	ולב העלם
of the young man,	*ha-e-lem*	
would beat no more.	*cha-dal le-fa-am.*	חדל לפעם

Falling off a horse: (Colonial Jewish Cemetery, Newport, RI)
Note the monument only indicates that he fell. However, his obituary fills in that he fell from a horse!

In memory
of
Abraham Minis, Esquire,
of Savannah, in the state of Georgia,
who
departed this life at Newport
on 29th Aug. 1801,
aged 23 years, 6 months
and 14 days.

...

This inestimable young gentleman **fell a
victim in the bloom of life to the accidental
fracture of a leg,**
and died universally beloved, esteemed and lamented.

Murdered:

He was laid lifeless	*Na-fal sha-dud*	נפל שדוד
(cf. Ju. 5:27)		
by the hands of	*bi-dei*	בידי מרצח
a murderer	*me-ra-tsei-ach*	

- - - - -

Trampled:

OUR BELOVED SON
HAROLD A.
BORN JAN. 17, 1913
RUN OVER BY A TEAM
DIED OF INJURIES
AUG. 4, 1916
תנצבה

STINEMAN

Beth Joseph 2, Woburn, MA

Patriotism

The largest single category of monument epitaphs describing the cause of death is war casualties. The following is transcribed from a weathered marble obelisk showing the obvious pride of Jacob Scharf's family.

<u>Translation</u>

פ' ✡ נ'

Here lies	
our beloved son,	בננו היקר
the young man,	הבחור
Jacob	יעקב
son of Mr.	בר'
Ze-eiv Wolf (William)	זאב וואלף
Born 14 Shevat	נולד יד שבט
in the year 5659 (1899)	שנת תרנט
and died 4 Nisan	וני ד ניסן
in the year of 5678 (1918)	שנת תרעח
He gave his life for	נפשו מסר בעד
his country, the United States	ארצו ארי הברית
and he died like a hero	ונפל כגבור
in the field of battle	בשדה המלחמה
in the country of France.	במדינת צרפת

One of the first
to serve his contry(sic)
and the first
to give his life
in the
Great World War
from Everett Mass.

Austrian Cemetery Association, Woburn, MA

127

Heroism

Below on the left is the entire monument. On the right is a close up of the inscription commemorating the heroism of Abraham Kolp.

Beth Emeth, Albany

TO THE MEMORY OF
ABRAHAM KOLP
BORN MAY 21ST 1846
FOR SACRIFICING HIS LIFE WHILE
ENDEAVORING TO SAVE FROM
DROWNING
DAVID LOEWENTHAL
ON THE 26TH DAY OF JUNE 1864

ERECTED BY HIS FRIENDS

Section 2, Chapter 11. Politically Incorrect

Murdered by an American Negro
On the left is a rubbing of the monument. On the right is a photo of it. A transcription follows on the right with a translation on the left:

Old Jewish Cemetery, Waldheim Cemetery, Forest Park, IL

A monument to the soul of

our beloved father

who was murdered by the hands of

American Negroes[14].

[15]Our rabbi and teacher, Monis son of Mr.

Meshulem Mordechai

died 11 Tishri

5671, May his soul be bound
up in the bonds of the living.

ציון לנפש

אבינו היקר

שנהרג בידי

שחורי אמעריקי

מוה מנות בר

משולם מרדכי

נפטר יא תשרי

תרעא תנצבה

OUR BELOVED
FATHER
MORRIS
LIPSHITZ
DIED OCT. 14, 1910
AGED 53 YEARS
REST IN PEACE

On the surface of things, this may appear to be just politically incorrect by today's standards. However, in dis-
cussing the tombstone with the deceased's great-grandson,
it seems that Morris was a peddler in Chicago. Apparently, there were zone boundaries for peddlers and those
boundaries were enforced by gangs. In Morris's case, he
encroached on an area where the gang of blacks murdered
him to "make an example" for any other enterprising
peddlers.

---

[14] "Large print" for *American Negro* is author's emphasis.

[15] מוה which is usually translated as "Our rabbi and teacher" is sometimes used as a generic honorific. I have no reason to believe that
Morris Lipshitz was a Rabbi.

130

Egyptian Revival Architecture
The use of the obelisk, very popular in mid-19th century American cemeteries, also became popular in Jewish cemeteries. The obelisks of the Touro family are shown below. However, the obelisk is representative of the rays of the Egyptian Sun God, "Aton."

Colonial Jewish Cemetery, Newport, RI

The Gates of the Colonial Jewish Cemetery, Newport, RI shown next are in "Egyptian Revival Architecture." The winged-globe was interpreted to be a symbol of divine protection. The wings were the protecting wings of God. The globe represented the sun, the source of life and a major deity in the Egyptian culture. To the left and right are upside-down torches. They symbolized either extinguished light or light for the underworld.

Just to the left and just to the right of the main gate are obelisks. Twice a day in their morning and evening services, religious Jews, remember the Exodus from the horrors of slavery in Egypt. There is a fascinating irony to the choice of "Egyptian Revival Architecture" architecture in a Jewish cemetery! (Although there are some who justify the sun and sun's rays by citing Malachi 3:20. "But to you who

131

fear My name, the **sun** of righteousness shall arise with healing in its wings; ...")

Detail of Winged Globe

Colonial Jewish Cemetery, Newport, RI

Bragging?

The assumption of prudishness of a previous generation is shattered as we see the following inscription on the 1789 monument of Rachel Lopez (Colonial Jewish Cemetery, Newport, RI).

Sacred is this Marble here Erected in Memory of
Mrs. Rachel Lopez, the Beloved Consort of David Lopez, Jun.
...
on the 4th of Elul A. M. 5549, Corresponding to the 26th of August 1789 A E 31.
Endued with all the Excellencies of the Amiable Woman, her span of life, tho short, was employed in the exercise of every gentle Virtue. **Exemplary for conjugal affection she lived an ornament to her sex,** In Friendship, Constant and sincere,
the milk of human kindness filled her peaceful breast
and resignation marked her faith in God: thus in life
was she beloved and admired, in death lamented and revered.

Homosexuality

The most common epitaph referring to a heterosexual couple is the quotation from 2 Samuel 1:23. It is spelled out and translated next. Below that, an example is shown.

Beloved and cherished,	הנאהבים והנעימים
in life, and in death,	בחייהם ובמותם
they were not parted.	לא נפרדו

Temple Beth Abraham, Nashua, NH

The gay community has been accepted within Reform Judaism. Hebrew Union College-Jewish Institute of Religion (HUC-JIR) the major Reform seminary in the world, began ordaining openly gay people as rabbis by the 1980's. The more traditional branches of Judaism are not there yet.

The context of the quoted passage deals specifically with the love between David and Jonathan. The gay community has often cited this passage to suggest that David and Jonathan were lovers in more than a platonic sense. Given traditional Judaism's hang-up with respect to homosexuality, it is interesting that this text is not only acceptable in traditional cemeteries: it is popular!

Name Choice

The photo below shows the monument of Adolph Ginsberg. To those looking at names in the wake of the Holocaust, seeing a Jew named Adolph is a bit shocking.

But it is true: prior to the holocaust, Adolph used to be a popular first name among Jews.

Minneapolis Hebrew, Minneapolis, MN

In a similar fashion, Ishmael was a popular Jewish name prior to the rise of Islamic oppression and as more Christians convert to Judaism, there are Jews named, "Chris."

Sometimes, improper names happen, by what I can only surmise to be an error. I have never met a Jew with the Hebrew name עשו, Esau. Esau, the brother of Jacob, was rabbinically categorized as a villain and yet, the following clearly shows, the name of the deceased as: Isaac Chayim son of Esau: יצחק חיים בן עשו.

Beech Street Cemeteries, Manchester, NH

I am reasonably sure this is a mistake, but how does this happen? Often, people know their Hebrew (or Yiddish) name only phonetically in English and I suspect that he (or his family) reported his father's name to the monument

134

manufacturer as "Issa." In trying to transliterate the English phonetic sound to Yiddish or Hebrew, a mistake was made. I suspect that if birth records were available, one would learn that "Issa" was a diminutive of either Isaiah or Israel.

Who or What is an Inscription About?

The following is the most outrageous inscription I've ever encountered. Inscriptions tend to tell us about the deceased's relationship with the living or something about the life of the deceased.

What follows, is a full-fledged diatribe against his wife. While I am reluctant to be judgmental, in this case, I will be! This inscription is just plain inappropriate, even if it is true. On the other hand, if Mr. Harband wanted his tomb-stone to be noticed, this would certainly accomplish that.

In case the photograph isn't completely clear, what follows is a full transcript:

135

MY WIFE ELEANOR ARTHUR
OF QUEENS, N.Y. LIVED LIKE
A PRINCESS FOR 20 YEARS
TRAVELING THE WORLD WITH
THE BEST OF EVERYTHING.
WHEN I WENT BLIND
SHE TRIED TO POISON ME,
TOOK ALL MY MONEY,
AND ALL MY MEDICATION AND
LEFT ME IN THE DARK
ALONE AND SICK.
IT'S A MIRACLE I ESCAPED.
I WON'T SEE HER IN HEAVEN
BECAUSE SHE IS SURELY
GOING TO HELL!

Wow! As with several of the other totally politically incorrect monuments, I am choosing to omit its location. But I offer a few observations supported only by logic and hypothesis:

1. As of 2009, if Mr. Harband were still alive, he would be over 90-years old. Mr. Harband is obviously a very angry man! It is possible that he has passed on and had so alienated those close to him that no one bothered to fill in the remainder of the inscription.

2. It is possible that he posted this as a billboard which will be replaced with something more appropriate when he actually passes on. In the grand scheme of things, it's an easy and economical way to advertise a hostile message. An inscription like this though, is a great example of why cemeteries need to have some editing controls!

3. Anyone who has worked in the "helping professions" knows that there are two sides to every story and I would surely be curious to hear what his wife might have had to say!

4. And lastly, sometimes old-age is accompanied by dementia and paranoia. It could be his disease we are hearing.

New York – Boston Rivalries
Anyone who lives in the northeast is aware of the legendary sports rivalries between the Boston and New York City, so to see a Boston logo and a New York logo on the same monument gives an initial visceral reaction!

However, before 1960, there was no professional football franchise and until the American Football League became respectable in the late 60's, many in New England maintained their allegiance to the New York Football Giants. So this inscription falls into the category of acceptable in its day, but a bit shocking as a viewer of the inscription ca. 2010.

Beth David Memorial Gardens, Hollywood, FL

137

Moslems and Jews

Common wisdom would have it that Moslems and Jews don't get along. The vast majority of Jews and organized Judaism has no problem sharing the world with Moslems and there is no organization in the Jewish world that advocates unprovoked attacks on Moslems.

On the other hand, Islamists are repeatedly quoted as advocating violence against Americans and Jews in the name of Islam.

The following tombstones adjacent to each other are similar in design, both with photos engraved and appropriate religious symbolism. It clearly indicates that the potential to spend time together in peace is possible in death and leaves hope that perhaps in life too.

Forest Hills, Boston, MA

138

Section 2, Chapter 12. What are these about?

Where

Many monuments include place names where a person was born or where he/she died. However, this one leaves me asking, "If I didn't know where this monument was, how would I find it. And if I did, what new information is this inscription giving me?" Regardless, the following made it clear exactly where in the cemetery the viewer was standing. (Chelsea Chevra Kadisha, Woburn, MA.)

Buried in row 2, position 18   נקברה בשורה ב", נ" 18

Erected by his daughter ...

The monument shown next is a standard mix of Hebrew and English.

Anshe Lebovitz, Woburn, MA

However, at the bottom of the monument is the inscription, "Erected by his daughter ... ." and at the top the same statement is inscribed in Yiddish.

ערעטער באי ... ... זיין טאכטער

Monument inscriptions don't generally refer to the actions of the living. Are we being let in on a family feud? Perhaps her father was a difficult person who was known not to get along with his daughter. Was this statement made by her to quell gossip and to let others know that she had made peace with her father? Or perhaps there was a brother or other siblings who were unwilling to share the expenses.

When Children Come Between Their Parents
The beautiful and tall triple monument is shown completely in the inset on the left. The more detailed inscriptions, shown to the right, have father on the left, mother on the right and daughter in the middle. It is relatively common to have parents include a young unmarried child, in this case, Henrietta, age 18, on a triple headstone. However, the child is usually on the left or right. A few other noteworthy observations:
 - Mary outlived both husband and daughter for over 40-years. As such, the monument manufacturer did a wonderful job matching fonts.
 - There appears to be a place where a cameo photo was included when the original monument was placed. See the section on "Monument Art" for more on cameo photos.

Minneapolis Hebrew, Minneapolis, MN

Oops. A Footnote

Bernard Borkin passes away and his epitaph reads, "BE-LOVED HUSBAND DEVOTED FATHER AND SON." It would seem that after the fact, Bernard's sibling felt slighted to an extreme! Evidence for this is the size of the letters "AND" linking the footstone to the bottom of the headstone! The footstone-footnote reads "AND BELOVED BROTHER."

(from Cedar Park, Paramus, NJ)

Gibberish 1: Random Letters

Since most monument manufacturers do not know Hebrew, lettering is generally laid out using a lettering chart in which each Hebrew letter is numbered.

Example:

1	2	3	4	5	6	7	8	9	10	11	12
א	ב	ג	ד	ה	ו	ז	ח	ט	י	כ	ך

To have the name, Tuviah (טוביה), inscribed in Hebrew, the following data would be supplied to the monument maker:

5 10 2 6 9

The problem is: what if the lettering chart used by the manufacturer is different from the one used by the person who laid out the monument? Editing is much easier if the

141

readers understand what they are writing. But regardless of how it happened, the collection of Hebrew letters on the monument that follows might as well have been random letters.

IN LOVING MEMORY
LEONARD
MEYERS
NOV. 18, 1920 – JUNE 4, 2006

Bnai Brith, Peabody, MA

דְחכלִפְדְחב דְדב בחאכ

Gibberish 2 – Off by a Century and Backwards

Checking the common calendar dates from the monument below, July 15, 1885 corresponds to Av 3, 5645 and March 8, 1956 corresponds to Adar 25, 5716.

If one is clever enough to reverse the last line on the monument, we can extract: "3 Av 5755 – 35 (sic – 25) Adaba (sic – Adar) 5816." And therein lies another problem. A little knowledge is dangerous! Was the numbering chart data entered left to right or right to left? In this case, the supplier of the data did it one way and the monument manufacturer did it the other. Regardless of whom we blame for the errors, if we believe the Hebrew, Clara was buried alive and will be with us until March 13, 2056.

Mt. Nebo, Miami, FL

A Sphere and a Bench

The magnificent monument shown next has beauty and a serious aspect of the life of the deceased on the headstone. The footstone is stylized as a bench and provides us with insight into the lighter side of the deceased with many of the sayings (such as "page 26") being totally insider concepts:

The complete inscriptions are transcribed below:

Sphere:
  In every moment there is a reason to carry on.

Bench:
Front:
  Just put it on the card
  Courageous
  You can shower at my house
Left:
  Don't worry
Top:
  If you could have only one friend …
Back:
  Livin' Proof
  I'll be there in 5 minutes.
Right:
  Page 26

United Jewish Brotherhood, Minneapolis, MN

Section 3: In Summary
Chapter 1: Where Reality and the Theoretical Diverge:

The truth is, that when it comes to cemeteries, for every rule, there is an exception (or better yet, thousands of exceptions.) While many of the entries in previous chapters were unique, each of the entries in this chapter is merely a paradigm for many similar examples:

Question: Aren't Jewish tombstones generally simple[16]?
Reason: Proverbs 22:2: The rich and poor meet together (in death).
Reality:

Colma, CA

- - - - -

---

[16] Op. cit. Kolatch, Page 223

Question: Why is there objection to burying the dead in mausoleums[17]?

Reason: Burial requires that the coffin be covered by earth.

Reality:

Levi-Strauss Mausoleum, Colma, CA

- - - - -

Question: Why is cremation prohibited[18]?

Reason: Traditional Jewish texts look at the Ezekiel story of the "dry bones" (Ezekiel 37:1-14) as the paradigm for the resurrection of the dead. With cremation, there are no remaining bones that could be resurrected.

Reality:

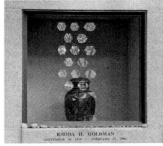

Cremation urn in the Goldman Mausoleum, Colma, CA

- - - - -

---

[17] Ibid.

[18] *A Field Guide to Visiting a Jewish Cemetery*, by Rabbi Joshua Segal, ©2005, JCP, LLC, NH. Pg. 17

146

Question: Why has there been a strong objection to erecting an iron gate or railing around a grave[19]?
Reason: It is demeaning to poor families who can't afford such luxuries.
Reality:

Crawford Street Shul Cemetery, Baker St., W. Roxbury

- - - - -

Question: Why should eulogies (and by extension, cemetery inscriptions) focus on the good?
Reason: To evoke positive memories of the deceased[20].
Reality: The following inscription is clearly a mixed bag:

TOO LATE
    TOO SOON
A NURTURING SUN
    A FRIGID MOON
ALPHA TO OMEGA
    SHE LEFT GOLDEN WORDS
    SHE LEFT EARTHY TURDS
APPLAUDED, HISSED,
    SHE'LL BE MISSED.

Blossom Hill, Temple Beth Jacob, Concord, NH

---

[19] Op. cit. Kolatch pg. 225
[20] BT, Shabbat 153a, inter alia

Question: Why should the wording on a monument be concise[21]?

Reason: It is consistent with the idea that every aspect of a burial should be simple.

Reality:

Temple Beth Abraham, Nashua NH

Acrostics are common in Jewish literature and liturgy. In this example, her name, אסתר רחל, is spelled out vertically in the rightmost column in majuscule script. The major theme of this acrostic is emphasis on traditional women's virtues: love of family and love of community. But the key point: it is anything but concise!

---

[21] Op. cit. Kolatch pg. 225

Here lies	פ'נ
Our beloved, modest and honorable mother.	אֱמנו היקרה הצנועה והכבודה
Her goodness is hidden from the eyes.	סתרה טובותיה לעניים
Torah was beloved to her.	תורה בלבה חמדה
Many ye-shi-vot[22] will remember her goodness.	רב בתי ישיבות לטוב יזכרוה
Many friends encountered her during her life.	רבות רעות פגעו בה בחייה
She was passionate about the well-being of her children.	חשקה נפשה לראות טוב על ילדיה
To do only goodness and righteousness, she commanded her son and her daughters.	לעשות אך טוב וחסד צותה לבנה ולבנותיה
Esther Rachel daughter of Mr. Kalman Mirsky	אסתר רחל בת ר' קלמן מירסקי
Day 11 of Si-van	יום י'א סיון
5691 Let her soul be bound up in the bonds of the living.	ת'ר'צ'א' תנ'צ'ב'ה'

- - - - -

Question: Why should superlatives not be used on monument inscriptions[23]?

Reason: The works of one's life should be their monument.

Reality: Superlatives, short and long, abound!

DR. JACOB GRUNBAUM
MAR. 21, 1906 — JUNE 25, 1982
PHYSICIAN OF RARE COMPASSION
יעקב שלמה צבי
בן אפרים פישל
נפטר ד" תמוז תשמ"ב
ת נ' צ' ב' ה'

Adath Israel, Massena, NY

---

[22] *Ye-shi-vot* are places for advanced Jewish studies.
[23] Op. cit. Kolatch pg. 225

149

Superlative underlined:

A physician of <u>rare</u> compassion (shown above)

Common rabbinic superlative:

The <u>sainted</u> Rabbi   הרב הצדיק   הרה"צ

- - - - -

Question: Why does Jewish Law prohibit engraving the human likeness on tombstones[24]?

Reason: Second commandment (Exodus 20:4): "You shall not make for you any engraved image, ..."[25]

Reality:

Adath Israel, Massena, NY

- - - - -

Question: Why are non-Jewish symbols not permitted in a Jewish cemetery?

Reason: There are many secular and non-denominational cemeteries that allow for this. The decorum/rules enforced in many Jewish cemeteries is: no non-Jews can be buried in a Jewish cemetery. As mixed marriage has increased, many Jewish cemeteries have sections where non-Jewish spouses can be buried but no non-Jewish symbolism is permitted.

Reality: See any of the examples in Section 2, Chapter 5, titled, "In a Jewish Cemetery?"

---

[24] Op. cit. Kolatch pg. 228

[25] Note that human likenesses such as the Cameo photos shown in other chapters are produced chemically and as such are not in the category of "graven image."

150

Section 3: Chapter 2: Debunking Some Jewish Myths with a Lighter Look at Tombstones

Dietary Laws – Unkosher or what?

Many people know virtually nothing about Judaism. But if they know anything, often it is that Jews follow a set of dietary laws than involve abstention from eating pork products and shellfish. The use of mollusk shells has mythological (non-Jewish) origins as a symbol of life and resurrection. However, it is seen more frequently than one might expect in a Jewish cemetery. Sometimes the shells are incorporated into the monument and sometimes they are left like pebbles. The truth is, the use of non-kosher animals for jewelry and ritual decoration is perfectly acceptable, with many a Torah scroll roller being decorated with turtle shell, ivory[26], or mother-of-pearl, all of which are from non-kosher animals.

Menorah Garden, Fort Lauderdale, FL

- - - - -

In the tombstones shown below, Moses is often considered a Jewish last name, or at the very least, a name associated with Judaism. However, from the crosses on this tombstone, it is clear that this Moses isn't Jewish. "Ham," on the other hand, is a relatively common Chinese surname. But somehow, these two monuments together, just didn't seem to be quite kosher.

---

[26] Note that new ivory ornaments are not made due to endangered species laws, not Jewish laws. But there are many old Torah scrolls which predate these laws with beautiful ivory ornaments.

151

Forest Hills, Boston, MA

- - - - -

As long as the subject is names, there are many Biblical first names that were very common among Christians. Biblical names, such as Phineas, Ebenezer, Obadiah, Hepzibah and Israel appear frequently on 18th and 19th century church yard tombstones, but not in more recent ones. Israel has remained a common first name among Jews. The following, on Mt. Desert Island Street, Bar Harbor, ME is not a Jewish cemetery and Mr. Ash was not Jewish. However, since the subject of this chapter is *kashrut*, ISRAEL H.ASH seemed too good to pass up!

Judaism: Race or Religion

The concept of "political correctness" emerged in earnest in the late 20th century. Up until then one could routinely experience racial, religious and gender insensitive comments in polite company. Judaism got a double whammy. Jews were attacked both as religion and race! The truth is, Judaism is a religion and a culture: not a race. The proof is simple. A non-Jew can convert to Judaism. A person can't convert from one race to another[27]. There are black Jews both by birth, from Ethiopian descent (and elsewhere) as well as by conversion.

There are however, "Jews of color" who are totally Caucasian and following the comedic rule of three, only three are presented below:

Gray:

Kopiagorod, Baker Street, West Roxbury, MA

---

[27] Although whenever I say that in a class, one of my teenage students invariably says, "What about Michael Jackson?"

153

Brown:

דוב בער ב"ר יהודה אריה
BEN B. BROWN
NOV. 4. 1903 – NOV. 7. 1967

תנ'צב'ה

Adath Israel, Massena, NY

Green:

האשה מריה גימצל
בת ר' ישראל יעקב
כ"ט שבט תש"ד
תנצב'ה
MY BELOVED MOTHER
IDA GREEN
DIED JAN. 30 1947
AGE 61

Kopiagorod, Baker Street, West Roxbury, MA

Note: Others options include, but are not limited to: Red (Roit), White, Blau (Blue), Gold, Black, Silver, etc.

154

Ethnic Stereotypes
Jewish Mother #1
There are some parents who live vicariously through their children. One Jewish mother stereotype is the idea that every Jewish mother wants their son to grow up to be a doctor (i.e. physician - not PhD or dentist, etc.) The following tombstone takes the concept to the grave where the epitaph only reads:

DORA OSTROFSKY
MOTHER OF DOCTOR
MORRIS OSTROFSKY
DIED ...

Beth Shalom, Pittsburgh, PA

Jewish Mother #2
Ethnic stereotypes, like a few words of a quotation, can often tell volumes. We have next, a "*Yiddishe momma.*"

Mt. Nebo, Miami, FL

And following our "*Yiddishe mama,*" we have a 78 year-old man whose epitaph characterizes him only as "A NICE JEWISH BOY." There are many "strong alpha males" among Jews. But none-the-less, the image of the "momma's boy" is a Jewish ethnic stereotype which has tenaciously held on.

155

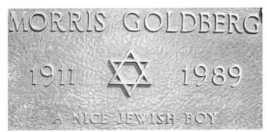
Menorah Garden, Fort Lauderdale, FL

Jews and Money
The idea that "Jews are moneyed" probably evolves from the Middle Ages when Jews, by virtue of government restrictions, were often forced into the role of money-lenders. And money lenders often need to appropriate the collateral on a loan when the debtor fails to pay the money lender. Lenders are never the sympathetic characters.

The early Jewish immigrants to America often became successful shop keepers and business people. The anti-Semites would have you believe that this was an ethnic thing. The truth is, the Jew had to make it some way, since the factories and mines would often discriminate against Jews

Jay Leno has done a bit for years where he combines two last names to tell a story about a wedding announcement in the newspaper. The "Better – Gold" family seems to fit this category!

Mt. Nebo, Miami, FL

Jews and Boxing

One of the methods by which minorities became mainstream Americans was through sports such as boxing. Jewish immigrants in the early 20th century were very active in the world of boxing. Two of the most famous Jewish boxers were Maxie Rosenbloom, world light-heavy weight champion from 1932-4; and Barney Ross, World War II hero as well as a great boxer. For the early Jewish influence of the Jewish world of boxing where "one chap belts the other," I offer: BELT – CHAPMAN.

New Tifferet Israel, Everett, MA

The Religion of Law, not Love

If a lie is repeated often enough, it is believed to be true. The myth that Christianity is "the religion of love" and Judaism is "the religion of law," is one of those myths. Some suggest the reason cited for this myth is *lex talionis*, the passage of the Bible that includes "an eye for an eye" (Exodus 21:23ff) versus the "turn the other cheek" as stated in the Christian's Bible (Matthew 5:39). The fact is, the "an eye for an eye" passage was created at a time when a peasant maimed a nobleman, the peasant and his entire

157

family might be wiped out, whereas if a nobleman maimed a peasant, there might be no punishment what-so-ever. It was a statement of equality under the law and in no way an absence of love.

However, 'nough (Knopf) on the subject of love.

Center Street, West Roxbury, MA

Section 3, Chapter 3. Mine is bigger Than Yours

The following is the translation of a paragraph of the Babylonian Talmud: Baba Matsia 84a, Soncino Edition, copyright 1962:

> Rabbi Johanan said, "The waist of Rabbi Ishmael son of Rabbi Jose was as a bottle of nine kavs capacity. Rav Pappa said, "Rabbi Johanan's waist was as a bottle containing five kavs"; others say, "three kavs." That of Rav Pappa himself was as [large as] the wicker-work baskets of Harpania (A rich agricultural town in the Mesene district South of Babylon, famous for its manufacture of large baskets made of fibers of palm leaves).

The Soncino translation was known for its prudishness. A more accurate translation of the text was offered by William Novak and Moshe Waldoks[28].

> Rabbi Johanan said, "Rabbi Ishmael's penis was like a wineskin of nine kavs' capacity." Rav Pappa said, "Rabbi Johanan's penis was like a wineskin of five kavs' capacity." Some report him as giving the measurement of "three kavs' capacity." And what about Rav Pappa himself? His penis was like Harpanian jug.

Somehow, the students of the rabbis found it worthy of analysis to compare the relative attributes of their rabbi's genitals! Perhaps, this is comparable to a bunch of young boys arguing, "My dad can beat up yours!"

This kind of "mine is bigger or better than yours" mentality plays out in the cemeteries, too. Following the death of Isaac M. Wise, considered the founder of Reform

---

[28] "The Big Book of Jewish Humor", by William Novak and Moshe Waldoks, copyright 1981, Harper and Row, NY. Page 265.

Judaism in America, his congregation honored him with the following tombstone. (Walnut Hills, Cincinnati, OH)

At a time when small markers were available from Sears for less than $10, the fact that I. M. Wise's was documented as having cost $750[29] might have raised some eyebrows. In today's world, an obelisk of this size (perhaps 40-feet in height) would cost in the neighborhood of $100,000, and most newer cemeteries do not even allow monuments to be that big.

[29] Information from American Jewish Archives, Cincinnati, OH. See "Acknowledgements."

Sprince/Podolinsky (all photos in this section are from the Shara Tfilo Cemetery, Baker Street, West Roxbury, MA)

Both Rabbi Solomon Sprince and Mordechai Podolinsky died in 1929. Rabbi Sprince in May; Mordechai Podolinsky died in August. A cursory check of the names indicates that neither was particularly famous. Mordechai Podolinsky's obituary would have been in the Boston Jewish Advocate, but those issues from the second half of 1929 are not available. There was no reference to his passing in either the Boston Globe or Boston Post. As for Rabbi Sprince, his obituary[30] was quite small and only made page 5 of the "Boston Jewish Advocate." It is arguable that the inscriptions on his monument are longer than his obituary.

I assume that Mordechai Podolinsky was a successful businessman and Rabbi Sprince was a beloved rabbi within his community. The monuments are shown next, Rabbi Sprince's to the right:

---

[30] Boston Jewish Advocate, May 30, 1929, pg. 5

So why, in a very large cemetery, are there only two large monuments of this size[31]? Why are they back-to-back? Why is Rabbi Sprince's clearly in the category of "Our rabbi's memorial is better than your memorial"? Why are there no monuments of this style afterwards?

In the absence of easily findable data, I offer the following speculation, but first, a few observations:

1. Large monuments of this nature usually have extra lawn space associated with them. These both fill the entire plot.
2. The major inscriptions on the Podolinsky monument can be seen only in the two foot alley between the two monuments as shown next.

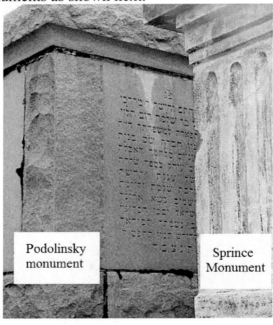

Podolinsky monument

Sprince Monument

---

[31] These two monuments may appear to be mausoleums, but they are not. In both cases, the bodies are buried below ground level. Details about this style of monument can be found in *A Field Guide to Visiting a Jewish Cemetery*, by Rabbi Joshua Segal, ©2005, JCP, LLC, NH. pp. 10-13

3. The Podolinsky monument includes both Mordechai and his wife, Riba. The Sprince monument is only for Rabbi Sprince. His wife's burial site is just to the left of his monument.
4. The spectacular front of the Sprince monument shown next, completely obscures and upstages the Podolinsky monument.

So, despite the fact that Rabbi Sprince pre-deceased Mordechai Podolinsky, my first conclusion is that Mordechai Podolinsky's monument was paid for by his estate and was placed first.

After the fact, the large monument in the cemetery became controversial. After it was placed, there was some regret that it was even allowed. A collection of Rabbi Sprince supporters said, "If so-and-so can have such a monument, we can do better for our beloved rabbi." So, I doubt that Rabbi Sprince or his estate paid for the Sprince monument.

The fact that there are no monuments of this size or style in the 80-years following is indicative that there was some pain and controversy. According to Riba Podolinsky's epitaph, she survived him by 30-years, passing in December 1959. It would be hard to imagine that there are no long-standing family resentments.

The Jewish Cemetery Association of MA (JCAM), who operate and maintain the cemetery confirm that monuments of this size are not permitted today, but are not sure when the rules might have changed to prohibit them.

Section 3: Chapter 4: The End

Ultimately, the cemetery monument is the end of the road physical world, but for Mel Blanc, the voice of Bugs Bunny, Porky Pig and so many more characters, turns "the end to most Warner Brothers cartoons" into his personal epitaph[32] as well as the end for this book!

Hollywood Memorial Park, CA

---

[32] That the quotation of a pig, namely Porky Pig, ("That's all folks") is in a Jewish cemetery is in itself funny!

Appendix A: A Monument Designer's Checklist

Preliminary
1. Get a copy of the bylaws of the cemetery in which you are considering obtaining plots.
2. Look around the cemetery at the monuments from the last 20-years. Many cemeteries have made rule changes in most cases due to maintenance related issues, so if there is a monument style or size that existed 50 or 100-years ago, it may no longer be allowed.
3. There are things that people want to include that might be considered an "insider joke." If it is something that could be misunderstood by a passer-by, you might consider using it in the context of Section 1, Chapter 9. titled, "Pebbles, Pebbles and More Pebbles."

- - - - -

Details:
1. Material for the monument

2. Shape of monument _____

3. Decorations or Art Work _____

4. Single or Multiple Widths _____

5. Fonts and Language _____

6. Hebrew Texts

a. Introductory Line

_____

b. Name Line

_____

_____

c. Date Line

_____

_____

d. Epitaph

_____

_____

_____

_____

_____

_____

_____

ת' נ' צ' ב' ה'

7. English Texts

  a. Introductory Line

  _____

  b. Name Line[33]

  _____

  _____

  c. Date Line

  _____

  _____

  d. Epitaph

---

[33] On a woman's grave, the genealogists will be very appreciative if you include the maiden name.

Appendix B: Glossary of Hebrew and Yiddishisms

Baubie, Bubbe, Bubbie, etc.: Grandma

Chachka: A knick knack

Chanukah: Jewish Holiday usually in the December that commemorates the survival of Judaism in the face of extreme Hellenistic pressure to assimilate.

Chanukiah: A candelabrum (menorah) that specifically has 9-branches and is used on Chanukah.

Chu-kat Ha-go-yim: Imitation of non-Jewish practices

Cohen: Someone who claims to be a direct descendant of the *ko-ha-nim*, כהנים, "the Biblical priests." *Ko-ha-nim* (priests) are given vestigial honors within Orthodox and Conservative synagogues.

Ei-shet Cha-yil: "A woman of valor, …". The Biblical description of the perfect wife. Proverbs 31:10ff.

Hanukah and many variants: See Chanukah

Kashrut: Jewish laws for maintaining kosher food; pertaining to keeping kosher

Ke-vod ha-meit: The honor of the deceased

Ko-ha-nim: plural of *Cohen* (*Ko-hein*)

Ko-hein: See Cohen.

Kosher: Mean "fit for use." It is usually used to refer to food that is fit to eat by those who observe Jewish dietary rules. "Not kosher" is used in colloquial English as an emphatic, "that's not right!"

Le-vi-im: plural of Levite

Levite: Someone who claims to be a direct descendant of Jacob's son, Levi, are called *le-vi-im*, לויים," the Levites." *Le-vi-im* (Levites) are given vestigial honors within Orthodox and Conservative synagogues

Magen David: A 6-pointed star, also knwn as a Jewish Star

Ma-tsei-vah: Hebrew for "monument."

Ma-tsei-vot: Plural for *Ma-tsei-vah*

Menorah: A candelabrum, usually used for ritual lighting of candles associated with Sabbath or a holiday.

Mitsvah: A commandment specified in or derived from the Bible.

Mitsvot: Plural of *Mitsvah*

Non-kosher: Unkosher – see Kosher

She-ma: Deut. 6:4ff. Judaism's most important prayer

Shul: Yiddish for synagogue

Unkosher: not kosher – see Kosher

Yad Vashem The name of the memorial to the Holocaust in Jerusalem which is based on Isaiah 56:5. It is often translated "a memorial and a name", but literally, "*Yad Vashem*" translates to "a hand and a name".

Yahrzeit: The anniversary of the day of death of a person.

Yeshiva (pl. Yeshivot): A Jewish Day School at any level from Grade School thru Graduate School

Yiddish: language of many Jews of East-European descent. It is a mixture of German and Hebrew written in the Hebrew alphabet

Yiddishe: Jewish, usually used to imply a warm cultural hominess

Zay-de: Grandpa

Appendix C: On Transliteration

Many Hebrew passages are presented in Hebrew, translation and in transliteration.

To be sure, transliteration is an inexact science. The transliteration formula in this book is that used in the mid-1970's publications of the liturgies of the Central Conference of American Rabbis. In the opinion of the author, this is the simplest method for pronouncing Hebrew, by those who really can't read Hebrew.

The transliteration formula for vowels is as follows:
1. **a** is pronounced as in b<u>a</u>t
2. **ai** is pronounced as in Th<u>ai</u>land
3. **e** is pronounced as in b<u>e</u>t
4. **ei** is pronounced as in v<u>ei</u>n
5. **i** is pronounced interchangeably as in m<u>e</u> or f<u>i</u>t
6. **o** is pronounced as in h<u>o</u>me
7. **u** is pronounced interchangeably as in fl<u>u</u>te or p<u>u</u>t

The transliteration formula for consonants is as follows:

1. The **ch** sound as in the English word **ch**ant <u>does not</u> exist in Hebrew. Whenever **ch** occurs in a transliteration, it is the gutteral sound as in <u>Ch</u>anuka.

2. The combination **ts** is pronounced as in the word ge<u>ts</u>. In English, this combination never occurs at the beginning of a word. Therefore, the English speaker, although familiar with the sound, often has trouble pronouncing it at the beginning of a word.

3. All other consonants are sounded as normal English pronunciation.

Cemetery Index
*: means – not a Jewish cemetery

United States

176

Subject Index
A through B

179

C

F through *Hoisl*

Materials through Mistakes

O through Politically Incorrect

W through Z

W

Y

Z